Vladimir Nabokov

With much love,
always.
Barbera.

Titles in the series Critical Lives present the work of leading cultural figures of the modern period. Each book explores the life of the artist, writer, philosopher or architect in question and relates it to their major works.

Vladimir Nabokov

Barbara Wyllie

REAKTION BOOKS

For my mum

Published by Reaktion Books Ltd
33 Great Sutton Street
London EC1V ODX, UK

www.reaktionbooks.co.uk

First published 2010

Printed and bound in Great Britain
by CPI Antony Rowe, Chippenham, Wiltshire

British Library Cataloguing in Publication Data
Wyllie, Barbara
    Vladimir Nabokov. – (Critical lives)
    1. Nabokov, Vladimir Vladimirovich, 1899–1977.
    2. Authors, American – 20th century – Biography.
    3. Authors, Russian – 20th century – Biography.
    I. Title II. Series
    813.5'4-DC22

    ISBN: 978 1 86189 660 5

Contents

Nabokov at his lectern, complete with supplies of index cards and pencils with rubbers on the end.

1

'Nothing will ever change, nobody will ever die'[1]

In the pre-dawn hours of 22 April 1899,[2] in a first-floor room of
a grand St Petersburg townhouse, Elena Nabokov gave birth to a
son. Vladimir Vladimirovich was the first of five children – Sergey
(1900), Olga (1903), Elena (1906) and Kirill (1911) – born into a
family of immense wealth and high social standing. His mother
was the daughter of Ivan Rukavishnikov, a millionaire philanthro-
pist. His father, Vladimir Dmitrievich (V. D.) Nabokov, came from
a long line of prominent noblemen that could be traced back to the
court of Ivan the Terrible and further still to a fourteenth-century
Tartar prince. A 'Gentleman of the Imperial Chamber', he trained as
a lawyer and lectured at the School of Jurisprudence in St Petersburg.
Renowned throughout Russia and Europe as a leading criminolo-
gist, he specialized in sexual crime, controversially campaigning
for the rights of homosexuals and the protection of children.
Vehemently opposed to capital punishment and all forms of social
and religious discrimination, he was an outspoken advocate of liberal reform, publishing regularly in the radical press both inside
and outside Russia.

The Nabokovs enjoyed a cultured and cosmopolitan life, with a
social network that included statesmen and generals, artists, writers,
actors, musicians and opera stars. Winters were spent at their opulent
home in St Petersburg, summers at their estate some 50 miles south
of the city. There they had three houses at their disposal, two that
had belonged to Elena's father – Vyra, which she inherited, and the

V. D. and Elena Nabokov, 1900.

mansion at Rozhdestveno, which now belonged to her brother Vasily (Uncle Ruka) – and the other, Batovo, which belonged to V. D.'s mother. All three properties were connected by the Orodezh river which led to the village of Vyra, where Elena's father had built three schools, a hospital, a public library and a theatre.

The entire estate resonated with the echoes of an illustrious past. The Imperial Russian family had spent many summers there, whilst Batovo had been the family home of the Decembrist leader and poet, Kondraty Ryleev. Ryleev was executed with four others for his part in the Decembrist uprising of 1825, and an avenue of trees in the park – 'The Alley of the Hanged' – was named in his honour. His ghost was said to haunt one of the rooms of the house. Rumour also had it that, five years earlier, Ryleev and Pushkin had fought a duel there. Pushkin, along with his seconds, was reported to have crossed the Rozhdestveno bridge that linked all three estates. He was later to use the postmaster's station in the nearby village of Vyra as the setting for one of his 1831 Belkin Tales.

The family's three-storey house in the heart of St Petersburg – no. 47, Bol'shaya Morskaya – also belonged to Elena. Located in an exclusive quarter known as the English Quay on the south side of

Vyra.

Batovo.

the Neva, it was one of a street of elegant mansions with Nevsky Prospekt at its east end, running along the Moyka Canal to the west, just a few blocks away from the Admiralty, St Isaac's Cathedral and the Mariinsky Palace. A fashionable art nouveau mansion, it had a side entrance for carriages and later, cars. The upper floor was set aside for the children and their servants, with bedrooms, dressing rooms, a music room and a study on the first floor, reception and dining rooms on the ground floor, and a library that doubled as a sports room, where V. D. Nabokov boxed, fenced and played billiards.

Brought up in the closeted comfort of an upper-class household, the Nabokov children spent much of their time with governesses and tutors, who were responsible both for their education and, particularly in the city, their recreation. They would be taken out tobogganing or ice-skating, to street markets and parties, to the theatre or the opera, but only in the countryside did they enjoy the privilege of absolute, exhilarating freedom. Long summer days were spent boating, swimming, riding, picnicking. Vladimir particularly loved the solitary thrill of exploring the grounds of

47 Bol´shaya Morskaya.

Vyra, with its tennis court, stables and pavilion, its carefully kept lawns, wild woods, meadows and marshland. His mother was especially fond of their country home, and encouraged him to notice, appreciate and mentally record the most precious details that made the place so magical to her. 'Vot zapomni', she would say to him, 'Now remember'.[3] She nurtured his visual memory from a very early age, fostering an acute sensory response to the many facets of colour and light generated by a handful of jewels, the play of sunshine through stained glass or the changing hues of trees and plants from spring to autumn. When Nabokov discovered his synaesthesia, which he referred to as 'coloured hearing', at the age of seven, she revealed to him that she too, had the gift, except the colours of her alphabet differed from his. She introduced him to the great Russian tradition of mushroom picking, whilst encouraging the fascination for butterflies he had inherited from his father, which was to become a lifelong passion.

Nabokov noticed his first butterfly in June 1906 – a swallowtail, which was captured and contained for just one night before it

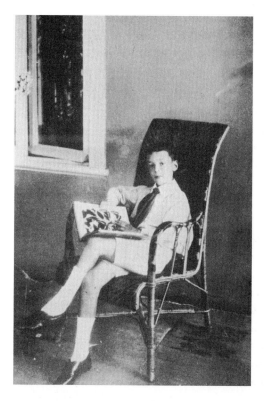

Nabokov with a butterfly book, 1907.

escaped.[4] Soon after, on finding a particularly 'spectacular' moth, his mother showed him how to kill it and pin it, but it wasn't until he was bedridden with an almost fatal bout of pneumonia in early 1907 that his interest became serious. Having been till then a prodigy with numbers, the severity of his fever caused him to lose completely his mathematical genius. Meanwhile, Elena surrounded her son's bed with butterfly books and paraphernalia such that 'the longing to describe a new species completely replaced that of discovering a new prime number'.[5]

Childhood illnesses also resulted in the revelation of another unusual attribute, Nabokov's clairvoyance. The deliria he frequently suffered would leave him in a 'strangely translucent' state of euphoric 'lightness', and in one instance he visualized in vivid detail a simultaneous event of which he could have had no know-ledge. This telepathy he shared with his mother, who would calmly describe her experiences of 'double sight, and little raps in the woodwork of tripod tables, and premonitions, and the feeling of the *déjà vu*'.[6] Although in much of Nabokov's fiction any organized or deliberate attempts to access the supernatural are presented as ludicrous, barren rituals, there is no question that such real-life experiences, no matter how ephemeral, were of great significance to him. He was later to confess that he was 'subject' to 'embarrass-ing qualms of superstition and that he [could] even be affected obsessively by a dream or a coincidence'.[7] Combined with his synaesthesia, which had already made him acutely aware of the 'leakings and drafts' that penetrated the not-so-solid walls of his consciousness,[8] these sensations informed what was to become an abiding preoccupation with 'other worlds' in his work. These experiences also happened to coincide with a growing interest in spiritualism in Russia, complemented by the investigations of Western thinkers such as William James, and expressed most potently in the burgeoning Symbolist movement in literature and art.

The Nabokov household was strongly Anglophile. Apart from the trappings of Edwardian English life acquired from Drew's English shop on Nevsky Prospekt, the Nabokov children spoke and read English before either French or their native tongue. Nabokov described himself as 'an English child',[9] brought up on fairy tales and Arthurian legends, the Golliwogg books of Florence Kate Upton, Captain Mayne Reid's Wild West adventures and the escapades of Buster Brown.[10] Their father, 'an expert on Dickens', would read aloud great 'chunks' to them, in English.[11] Vladimir became a prolific reader. He took full advantage of both his father's 10,000-volume library in St Petersburg and the library at Vyra,

Nabokov and his father, 1906.

which spilled across two rooms. His heroes were the Scarlet Pimpernel, Phileas Fogg and Sherlock Holmes. At the age of eleven he set himself the task of translating Mayne Reid's *The Headless Horseman* into French. At twelve, Nabokov's father introduced him to *his* favourite of the time, the philosopher/psychologist, William James, brother of American novelist Henry James. By the time he was fifteen, Nabokov had 'read or re-read all Tolstoy in Russian, all Shakespeare in English, and all Flaubert in French',[12] as well as, among others, Browning, Keats, Conrad, Kipling, Wilde, H. G. Wells, Edgar Allan Poe, Pushkin, Chekhov and Gogol.[13] His reading also extended to contemporary Russian poetry, to the Symbolists Blok, Voloshin, Bely and Bryusov, and Acmeists Gumilyov and Kuzmin. Encouraged by his mother, he amassed a substantial personal collection purchased mainly from Volf's bookshop on Nevsky Prospekt. 'Never was poetry so popular', he was later to comment, 'not even in Pushkin's days. I am a product of that period, I was bred in that atmosphere.'[14]

In 1911 Vladimir and Sergey were enrolled at St Petersburg's Tenishev School. Nabokov was a 'slender, well-proportioned boy with [an] expressive, lively face and intelligent probing eyes which glittered with sparks of mockery'.[15] He was also a stubborn non-conformist, refusing to 'join in', spurning clubs and societies, always opting to play in goal rather than on the pitch with the rest of the football team. Nabokov's detachment could well be interpreted as arrogance, but it is more indicative of his sense of simply not fitting in, and having no desire to. His exceptionally privileged upbringing had granted him a formidable self-sufficiency, confidence and personal autonomy, tempered by his father's persistent emphasis on the need to treat others with thoughtfulness and respect, dignity and humility. Throughout his life Nabokov's defence of social, personal and artistic freedom was unwavering, but the intense privacy he so carefully guarded and his reputation for dogmatism meant that he was often perceived as indifferent and aloof. When it came to treating others, however, even at the height of his fame, he was reported to be 'gentle, joking, generous, anxious never to offend or demand too much'.[16]

For much of his early childhood, Nabokov remained blissfully unaware of the increasingly dangerous and urgent battles his father was fighting in Russia's political arena. Since 1903, V. D. Nabokov had been a member of the St Petersburg duma, where he gained a reputation for vociferous criticism of social injustice. In April 1903 he published an article condemning the Kishinyov pogrom, accusing the police and the tsarist regime of anti-Semitism. During 1904, social and political tensions escalated throughout Russia, fuelled by its disastrous war with Japan, such that by early 1905 the situation in St Petersburg had reached crisis point, with strikes crippling the city. The gunning down of peaceful protesters attempting to deliver a petition at the Winter Palace on Sunday 22 January 1905 galvanized anti-tsarist feeling and triggered widespread social and political dissent. V. D. was one of the first to publicly denounce the Bloody Sunday massacre, demanding compensation for the victims' families. For this he was stripped of his court title and his post at the School of Jurisprudence, to which he responded by 'coolly advertis[ing] in the papers his court uniform for sale'.[17] His bravura stand was commendable, but he must have been aware that such outright provocation could invite serious repercussions. His new vulnerability, combined with the outrage of Bloody Sunday, which had occurred so horrifyingly close to home, convinced him that it would be safest to remove both himself and his family to Europe. Despite the risks, by the end of the summer his determined patriotism compelled him to return, and eventually it was Elena's nostalgia for her beloved country that brought his family back to Vyra that winter.[18] Ironically, where they had had a choice to abandon Russia at this stage in its history, some fourteen years later they were to have none. Nabokov later described 'that particular return' as 'my first *conscious* return', a 'rehearsal – not of the grand homecoming that will never take place, but of its constant dream in my long years of exile'.[19]

Back in St Petersburg, V. D. helped set up the Constitutional Democratic (CD) Party, also known as the Party of the People's Freedom, successfully campaigning for election to Russia's first parliament in March 1906. The political situation was still extremely unstable, with unrest spreading to the military, and by July the Duma had been dissolved. The CDs gathered in Vyborg, Finland, where they drew up a manifesto calling for widespread resistance to the government. This not only lost them their political rights but also provoked the extreme right wing into action. When a leading party member was assassinated, V. D. disappeared quickly, taking Elena to Holland – he was second on the reactionaries' hit list. In December 1907, V. D. stood trial for signing the Vyborg Manifesto. He was sentenced to three months' solitary confinement in St Petersburg's Kresty prison where, from May to August 1908, he wrote a series of articles on the Russian penal system and

V. D. Nabokov on his way to serve his sentence at Kresty Prison, 1908.

taught himself Italian, so that he could read Dante in the original. A bribed guard would smuggle notes out to Elena, written on toilet paper. In one, V. D. asked if there were any Speckled Woods at Vyra – 'Tell [Vladimir] that all I see in the prison yard are Brimstones and Cabbage Whites.'[20] On his return home the inhabitants of three local villages turned out to greet him.

The Vyborg episode heightened V. D.'s awareness of the precariousness of his own fate, and by 1911 his reputation was such that Elena could fill an album of political cartoons targeting him. During this year a situation arose which forced V. D., as a matter of honour, to deliberately tempt that fate. Insinuations erupted in the press, scandalizing him and his entire family. V. D. responded by demanding a retraction, with the condition that if none was made he would challenge the editor of the newspaper responsible to a duel. Vladimir saw one of the press accounts ridiculing his father, and was convinced that he would fight and almost certainly be killed. In the end the matter was resolved with an apology, but for Vladimir it came as the first and very stark realization of the fragility of his father's presence in his world.

Meanwhile, Vladimir's life continued to be one of endless enchantment and adventure. The critical summer of 1905 was spent travelling to Paris via the luxuriant Nord Express, and on to Beaulieu in the South of France and Milan. On the beach at Beaulieu he fell in love with a little Romanian girl. By the autumn, the family were in Wiesbaden, where he met his cousin, Yuri Rausch von Traubenberg, who was to become a close friend. Two years later, the children summered in Biarritz, where Nabokov fell in love again, this time with a Serbian girl called Zina, but it was not until 1909, on that same beach, that he claimed to experience 'the real thing'.[21] He and Claude Deprès decided to elope, taking with them Nabokov's butterfly net and Claude's fox terrier, but they only got as far as the cinema before they were caught.

From the summer of 1912, when not chasing butterflies, Nabokov would draw and paint, avidly, under the supervision of his new drawing master, Mstislav Dobuzhinsky, who was a major figure in the *Mir iskusstva* ('World of Art') movement.[22] Afternoons were spent acting out gunfights inspired by the stories of Mayne Reid and Fenimore Cooper with his cousin, Yuri. Eighteen months older than Nabokov, Yuri was sophisticated, dashing and recklessly heroic. At sixteen he produced an engraved silver cigarette case that had been given to him by a countess with whom he had spent three illicit nights. He went on to join the cavalry of Lieutenant General Denikin's White Guard, but was killed in the Crimea in 1919 making an impetuous lone charge on a Red Army machine-gun nest. Only three years earlier the boys had swapped clothes, Nabokov donning Yuri's uniform, and in mourning the loss of someone he had so admired, he was left with the feeling that it could so easily have been him lying in that field with his face smashed in by bullets. He was, after all, on the brink of joining up himself.

Although Nabokov had been writing verse in three languages since the age of nine or ten, it was not until he was fourteen that he produced the first poem that really counted. Decades later, he recalled the seminal moment as a flash of inspiration that came in the lull following a thunderstorm at Vyra. The scene emphasizes the elements he recognized as key to his artistic inspiration – the synchronization of an external phenomenon with an intensely felt subjective sensation, here the rhythm of rain drops with the beats of his heart set against shifting light and colours – but it also establishes the very personal significance of the location. It was in the same 'rainbow-windowed' pavilion where he had taken shelter that he was to meet his first love, Valentina Shulgin (Tamara in his autobiography), one year later.[23]

The hundreds of poems that Nabokov began composing with a 'numb fury' following this initial, epiphanic episode were 'hardly anything more than a sign [he] made of being alive, of passing or having passed, or hoping to pass, through certain intense human emotions'. What he did realize, very quickly, however, was that a poetic consciousness required the ability to think of 'several things at a time', to develop a 'manifold awareness' which could produce a kind of 'cosmic synchronisation', 'an instantaneous and transparent organism of events, of which [he] the poet [was] the nucleus'.[24]

By the summer of 1915 he had a muse, and that winter his first published poem, 'Autumn', appeared in the Tenishev School magazine. The following summer, encouraged by the acceptance of one of his poems (albeit 'as banal as a blue puddle in March') for publication in the 'distinguished' journal, *Vestnik Evropy* (*The Herald of Europe*),[25] he self-published a collection of 68 verses which he later referred to as 'juvenile stuff, quite devoid of merit and [which] ought never to have been put on sale'.[26] This opinion was harshly confirmed by the prominent Symbolist poet, Zinaida Gippius, who told V. D. Nabokov that his son would 'never, never be a writer'.[27]

Rozhdestveno, Nabokov's inheritance.

The People's Militia on patrol during the first days of the February Revolution in Petrograd, 1917.

By the autumn of 1916 his affair with Valentina was over. Nabokov returned to St Petersburg (now Petrograd) to the news that his uncle Ruka had died, leaving him the entirety of his vast estate, which included the palatial manor at Rozhdestveno and 2,000 acres of land, valued at several million dollars. Nabokov took full advantage of his new-found wealth and independence, embarking on a series of 'overlapping love affairs, some delightful, some sordid', ranging 'from one-night adventures to protracted involvements and dissimulations' but all 'with very meagre artistic results'.[28] Amongst these, however, was one serious and lasting romance with a 22-year-old Polish Jewish woman, Eva Lubrzynska. Nabokov sustained this relationship over the next three years, despite the cataclysmic forces that were to utterly transform their lives.

Meanwhile, Russia was buckling under the strain of yet another devastating and costly war. Since August 1914, the Russian army had been suffering heavy losses to German-allied forces along an

Eastern Front that stretched from the Black Sea in the south to the Baltic in the north. The expense of sustaining millions of troops in an increasingly futile conflict had brought Russia to the brink of economic collapse. By early 1917, initial patriotic fervour had been reduced to bitter disillusionment. February saw Petrograd once again in the grip of mass strikes and demonstrations. This time the army began to stand down, joining the ranks of protestors, and by the end of the month the city saw fierce fighting between revolutionaries and those still faithful to the tsar. Early in March, the Romanovs conceded defeat and V. D. Nabokov was called in to draft Nicholas II's letter of abdication. Over the next few months, he was to figure as a key player on the chaotic and ever-mutating political scene.

In the meantime, his eldest son was still at school, writing and publishing poetry, taking the train from Vyra to Petrograd to meet his new lover, Eva. That autumn he collaborated with a schoolmate, Andrey Balashov, on a joint volume of verse, *Two Paths*, which comprised a dozen of each of their poems. He was working on a new poem the day the Winter Palace was stormed by Bolshevik guards (his father narrowly escaped capture), and on into one of the bloodiest nights of the October Revolution. Completing a 90th line, he remarked on how 'fierce rifle fire and the foul crackle of a machine gun could be heard from the street':[29]

> Everything is sad,
> the pavements are scarlet with blood;
> gray ragtag people, insolently,
> have crawled out of their holes.
> They are screeching on street corners,
> and their rotten ravings terrify me.
> Their coarse palms bear slavery's
> indelible black trace.

Soldiers and students lying in wait for the police near the Moyka Canal in Petrograd, October 1917.

What they want is annihilation
of passions, longing, beauty.
'Freedom' is their pretext,
yet what is freer than a dream?[30]

Within weeks it was decided that the city was too dangerous for Vladimir and Sergey to remain. A family friend had offered them all refuge in the Crimea, and the boys left first, with the rest of the family following on soon after. As the brothers boarded their train at Nikolaevsky Station their father told them that, 'very possibly', he would never see them again.[31] Over the next two months, V. D.'s position became increasingly insecure, and in December he was arrested and briefly imprisoned by the Bolsheviks. On his release he made hasty arrangements to join his family. Vladimir marked his father's arrival with a poem, 'To Liberty':

Left to right: Vladimir, Kirill, Olga, Sergey and Elena Nabokov, 1918.

> your bloodstained elbow covering your eyes,
> once more deceived, you once again depart,
> and the old night, alas, remains behind.[32]

The Nabokovs found themselves amongst a stream of exiles escaping from the north. They were in familiar company, but Vladimir was keenly conscious of the strangeness of his new environment that seemed to him so un-Russian, a feeling made more intense by the occasional letters from his first love, Valentina, that found his way to him. Nevertheless, here he could write, compose chess problems – he had just begun to play seriously with his father – and hunt butterflies without constraint. He made several forays into the Crimean hills during the summer and autumn of 1918, collecting over 70 species of butterfly and more than 100 species of moth. These expeditions were not without their hazards – on one occasion he was arrested and interrogated by Bolshevik soldiers on suspicion of signalling to a British warship with his butterfly net.

In terms of his development as a writer, 1918 saw him produce his first verse play, *In Spring*, 'a lyrical something in one act',[33] set around a chess game, and several key poems.[34] 'In Radiant Autumn' deployed what were to become signature motifs of coloured hearing and coloured glass for the first time, 'The Fountain of Bakhchisaray (in memory of Pushkin)' revisited a poem Pushkin had written when he, too, was in exile in the Crimea, 'Yalta Pier' depicted the scene witnessed by German soldiers sent to retrieve the drowned victims of a recent Bolshevik attack, and a series of nine 'Angel' poems, designed, Nabokov argued, more as investigations of Byzantine imagery than as any attempt to explore Christian themes. He re-read *Crime and Punishment*, which caused him to revise his initial, favourable opinion of Dostoevsky, an opinion that he was not then to change again: 'Listening to his nightly howl, / God wondered: how can it really be / that everything I gave / was so frightful and complicated?'[35] He was also introduced to Andrey Bely's *Symbolism*, a collection of essays on versification written in 1910 which made a profound impact on his understanding and mastery of metre and rhyme. Taking Bely's principles, Nabokov formulated a system of analysis that matched the meticulous attention to detail he demon-strated in his categorization of butterfly species. Utilized with painstaking and deliberate care, it was a method which he was to uphold throughout his literary career, despite all challenges and attempts to undermine it.

In early 1919 Nabokov wrote a 430-line answer to Blok's new epic poem, 'The Twelve'. Set in Petrograd during a snowstorm, it follows a patrol of twelve Bolshevik soldiers who are likened to Christ's apostles. Nabokov's poem, 'The Two', is also set in winter and features a group of a dozen men but, rather than depicted as saviours, they are cast as violent aggressors. Twelve peasants attack an innocent couple in their home at the dead of night, forcing them to seek refuge in freezing woods where they perish from the cold. In order to further underline his condemnation of

Blok's celebration of the Revolution, and in an explicit gesture of defiance against the new Russia and allegiance to the old, Nabokov chose not to parody Blok's style but rather to deliberately echo that of Pushkin.

The Crimean peninsula had been a battleground between Russia and the German-allied Ottoman Empire throughout the First World War and was now a key arena of conflict in the Russian Civil War. Brief stability had been assured by German occupation following the treaty of Brest-Litovsk in March 1918, but by November the treaty was broken, and for a time the White Army took control of the region. Having been able to stay out of the limelight by masquerading as a doctor, V. D. Nabokov was quickly appointed Minister of Justice in the newly formed Crimean Regional Government, but the Whites were only able to hold on for a matter of months. By April 1919 the Bolsheviks had once again seized power.

V. D. took his family to Sebastopol where a route out of Russia could be secured. On 15 April they sailed out of the harbour on a Greek ship bound for Athens 'under wild machine-gun fire from the shore'. Nabokov remembered 'trying to concentrate, as we were zigzagging out of the bay, on a game of chess with my father', but

> the sense of leaving Russia was totally eclipsed by the agonizing thought that Reds or no Reds, letters from Tamara would be still coming, miraculously, and needlessly, to southern Crimea, and would search there for a fugitive addressee, and weakly flap about like bewildered butterflies set loose in an alien zone.

For many years after, Nabokov was to equate the loss of his country with 'the loss of my love'.[36]

The Nabokovs travelled to Paris and then on to London where they were greeted by V. D.'s brother, Konstantin, chargé d'affaires at the soon-to-be-obsolete Russian embassy. They rented rooms in a red-brick Victorian mansion block in Chelsea, overlooking a tree-lined square. Elena Nabokov was able to cover a year's rent by selling the jewels she had smuggled out of Russia in a tub of talcum powder. Her pearls paid the fees for two years at Cambridge University for her sons. Vladimir went up to Trinity College that autumn having spent much of his summer at parties and balls, where he foxtrotted with Anna Pavlova and reignited his romance with Eva Lubrzynska. His latest notebook of poetry featured a chess problem for every poem, and in September he composed his first but not especially startling lines in English.

At Cambridge, Vladimir promptly switched from zoology to French and Russian. Apart from a select group of English friends, which included Rab Butler, he gravitated towards his Russian peers – his room-mate Mikhail Kalashnikov (Eva Lubrzynska's brother), Pyotr Mrosovsky, Count Robert Louis Magawly-Cerati de Calry and Prince Nikita Romanov, upon whom he was to base the character Vadim in his 1931 novel, *Glory*. Outside lectures he would join his friends on the Cam, on the tennis courts or the football field – he was later to admit that playing in goal prevented him from ever visiting the university library – and in his second term was knocked

Nabokov and Robert de Calry on the Cam, 1920–21.

out during the semi-finals of the university boxing trials. He had girlfriends in Cambridge and London, and continued to see Eva, although by December 1920 she had married a fellow undergraduate. He later described his time there as 'a long series of awkwardness, mistakes, and every sort of failure and stupidity, including romantic'.[37] In the meantime, finding London too expensive, Nabokov's family had moved to Berlin, where V. D. was in the process of setting up a new daily émigré newspaper, *Rul´* (*The Rudder*), and what was to become one of the city's major Russian publishing houses, Slovo (The Word).

The Cambridge tripos held little appeal for Nabokov. Unsurprisingly, he found greater stimulation in pursuing his own interests which, apart from composing poetry, included publishing his first paper on butterflies – 'A Few Notes on Crimean Lepidoptera' appeared in the *Entomologist* in February 1920. His reading also drew him to the new English poets, Rupert Brooke, A. E. Housman and Walter de la Mare. He was now writing in English as well as Russian, and in November published two poems – 'Home', in the *Trinity Magazine*, and 'Remembrance', in the *English Review*:

> Like silent ships we two in darkness met,
> And when some day the poet's careless fame
> Shall breathe to you a half forgotten name–
> Soul of my song, I want you to regret.
>
> For you had Love. Out of my life you tore
> One shining page. I want, if we must part,
> Remembrance pale to quiver in your heart
> Like moonlit foam upon a windy shore.[38]

In that same month he saw his first poem published in *Rul´* under the pseudonym Cantab, alongside a story by Ivan Bunin. In January 1921 three more poems and a short story, 'The Wood-Sprite', appeared. Another new poem, 'Crimea', was included in the August issue of *Zhar-Ptitsa* (*The Firebird*), prompting Nabokov's first critical review and, following the death of Blok, tributes by both Vladimir and V. D. Nabokov were published together in *Rul´*.

Like the poem 'The Two', 'The Wood-Sprite' stands as a fierce indictment of the senseless violence and devastation wrought by the Russian Revolution and Civil War, but it is also a lament for a lost country and a stark depiction of the trauma of enforced exile. A creature traditionally perceived as both a benign and malevolent force, the wood-sprite is master of the forests, and it is through his eyes that the devastation of Russia's land and people is graphically presented. He appears to the writer/narrator in the dead of night, and vanishes just as mysteriously, leaving only the sensation of his icy touch and the 'wondrously subtle scent . . . of birch, of humid moss'.[39] The wood-sprite's loss takes on dimensions far greater than any human experience, and yet he also signifies a very particular loss to the narrator as one of the many aspects of a land that formed the source of his inspiration. The creature's voice dominates the story, preventing its dramatic potency from being undermined by nostalgic sentimentality, whilst his non-human perspective establishes an emotive distance from the horrors he describes, in turn magnifying their impact on nature, such that it is seen to have been violated in equal measure by the wages of death and destruction. This is further compounded by the extent to which the wood-sprite's demonic qualities and magical powers are utterly vitiated by the presence of true evil in the form of man. Nabokov's story plays with familiar fairytale conventions but also the supernatural which was to become a crucial element of the metaphysical dimension of his art.

Nabokov signed his story 'Vlad. Sirin'. Anxious not to be confused with or to impose upon his father's name, Nabokov's adoption of this pen-name, which became his literary identity in Russian émigré Europe, also afforded him a means of guarding his artistic

Sirin bird, Russia, early 18th century.

autonomy and personal anonymity. As a principle, too, the potential of a pseudonym for self-referential play held considerable appeal. For example, in 1921, using the names Dorian Vivalcomb and Vivian Calmbrood, Nabokov authored, respectively, a letter to his parents and his first English verse play, *The Wanderers*, whilst Vivian Badlook, Vivian Darkbloom and Adam von Librikov make appearances in *King, Queen, Knave*, *Lolita* and *Ada* (1928, 1955 and 1969). Most importantly, however, the name served as a readily identifiable emblem of his literary persona. In Russian folklore, the *sirin* is a fabulous bird of paradise, combining the body of an owl and the face of a beautiful woman which, like the Greek Sirens, would entrance mortals with its singing. Nabokov's choice of this evocative name encapsulated the essence of his creative identity and the purpose of his art – to enchant, to delight, and to succeed.[40]

Berlin was by now the centre of the Russian emigration in Europe, and V. D. Nabokov one of its best-respected personalities. He paid host to a range of White Russian refugees, including the novelist Aleksey Tolstoy, CD founder and former minister of foreign affairs Pavel Milyukov, theatre director Konstantin

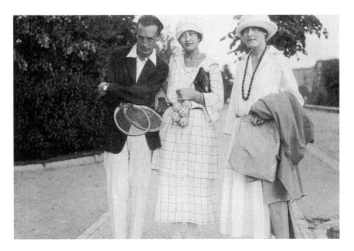

Nabokov with Svetlana Siewert (centre) and her sister, Berlin 1922.

Stanislavsky and his Moscow Art Theatre company, as well as the
actresses Olga Knipper (Chekhov's widow), Elena Polevitskaya and
Olga Gzovskaya. Vladimir was accused of having an affair with
Olga Gzovskaya, but managed to convince her jealous partner
that his suspicions were unfounded just as he was about to be
challenged to a duel. Shortly after he met another young Russian
émigré, sixteen-year-old Svetlana Siewert, cousin of his Cambridge
room-mate, Mikhail Kalashnikov. By the summer of 1922 they
would be engaged.

1922 was to be a momentous and tragic year for Nabokov. In
Berlin for the Easter vacation, he learnt that his father had invited
a former CD colleague, Pavel Milyukov, to give a lecture. On 28
March Milyukov stood before a crowd of over 1,000 at the Phil-
harmonic Hall. At ten o'clock, as he was finishing the first part of
his talk, a stranger emerged from the audience and started shooting.
In an instinctive move to protect his friend, V. D. Nabokov leapt to
his feet and tackled the gunman to the ground. Within moments a
second assailant appeared, shooting Vladimir Dmitrievich three

Nabokov in Berlin, summer 1922.

times in the back and killing him instantly. The assassins, Pyotr Shabelsky-Bork and Sergey Taboritsky, were members of an extreme right, pro-monarchist movement that held Milyukov responsible for the February revolution.[41] At their trial they claimed to know nothing of V. D. Nabokov or his political role in Russia over the past two decades, but were pleased to discover that, despite having missed their target, they had succeeded in murdering a prominent colleague.

The Nabokov family was devastated. Tributes poured in from the entire Russian community. On Easter Day, Vladimir published a new poem in his late father's newspaper: 'But if all the brooks sing anew of miracle . . . then you are in that song, you are in that gleam, you are alive.' Back in Cambridge for his final term, Vladimir wrote to his mother, 'at times it's all so oppressive I could go out of my mind – but I have to hide. There are things and feelings no one will ever find out'.[42]

On returning to Berlin that summer, Vladimir proposed to Svetlana Siewert. She felt she couldn't refuse him – he 'seemed

Nabokov's *Alice in Wonderland.*

so pitifully and uncharacteristically sad'.[43] Her parents agreed to
the marriage as long as Vladimir could demonstrate an ability to
provide for their daughter. That he was destined to be a writer was
confirmed when he began and ended his first and last job – in a
bank – in the space of three hours. Later that summer he was commissioned to translate *Alice in Wonderland* into Russian, for which
he was paid five US dollars. It is still considered to be the best Russian
version of Lewis Carroll's work. Between November 1922 and March
1923 he published a translation of Romain Rolland's *Colas Breugnon*
(the result of a bet he made with his father in 1920) and two collec-
tions of poetry – *The Empyrean Path* and *The Cluster*. This was not
enough to satisfy Svetlana's parents, however, and in January 1923
they insisted she break the engagement. For Nabokov the blow of

this rejection coming so soon after the loss of his father was almost unbearable. With Svetlana he claimed to have experienced 'the greatest happiness I ever had or will have'.[44] He threw himself into his work. From January 1923 he produced sixteen poems, including an epic of 850 lines, translations of English and French verse, a new short story, 'The Word', and a two-act play, *Death*. He also published his first chess problem in *Rul´* and appeared as an extra on a film set. In April he gave a reading of his work at a literary evening where he caught the attention of three ladies with his 'irresistibly attractive fine-featured, intelligent face',[45] one of whom he was to meet again, quite prophetically, very soon after.

Russian Jewish émigré Véra Slonim was 21 when she met Nabokov at a masked ball in May 1923. She had been following his rise as one of the most exciting young stars of the Berlin literary scene for over two years, and when she spotted him in the crowd she approached him, and talked to him about his poetry, all the while enigmatically refusing to show her face. Just three weeks later, in the South of France where he was spending the summer working as a farm labourer, Nabokov wrote a poem to mark their meeting. 'The Encounter' borrowed distinct images from Blok's 1906 'The Stranger', taking a line from his 'Incognita' – 'enchained by this strange proximity ...' – for its epigraph. In the meantime, Véra had sent him several letters. Eventually Nabokov replied: 'I am so unused to the idea of people ... understanding me ... that in the very first minutes of our meeting it seemed to me that this was a joke, a masquerade deception.'[46] At the end of June, in a very public and provocative move, Nabokov published 'The Encounter' in *Rul´* for which Véra was working as a writer and translator:

> The longing, and mystery, and delight. . . .
> as if from the swaying blackness
> of some slow-motion masquerade
> onto the bridge you came. . . .

Vladimir with Véra, 1923.

What did my heart discern in you?
how did you move me so? . . .

. . . Far off
I wander, and strain to hear
the movement of the stars above our encounter
And what if you are to be my fate . . .[47]

At the end of July, another poem, 'Song', appeared alongside Véra's
translation of an Edgar Allan Poe story, 'Silence'. This time, in an
unequivocally romantic gesture, Nabokov opened and closed his
verse with the word 'faith' – *vera*.

In the meantime, besides a number of other poems, Nabokov
had completed two new plays, *The Grandfather* and *The Pole*, and
had visited Marseilles, which inspired the short story, 'The Seaport'.
At the end of August he returned to Berlin, where he sought Véra
out. He discovered that they could have met many times. As a little
girl she regularly walked past the house on Bol´shaya Morskaya
and knew several of Nabokov's friends at the Tenishev School. As
a teenager she had spent a family holiday in a rented dacha near
Vyra, and only by chance missed bumping into him at the offices
of her father's Berlin publishing company, Orbis, where she worked.
He was taken aback by the instant physical, emotional, intellectual
and imaginative intimacy they shared, which extended to Véra's
ability also to see 'letters in color'.[48] In his poetry she assumed the
figure of the mysterious and elusive 'Beautiful Lady' from Blok's
early verse, which Nabokov, and his father, so admired. He was
convinced that they were fated to be together, and in April 1925
they married.

From the autumn of 1922 Germany began to be hit by catastrophic
inflation. Many émigrés left, and in October 1923 Vladimir's mother,
sisters and youngest brother moved to Prague. Sergey went to
Paris. Véra's father was ruined when Orbis went out of business,

and Nabokov was forced to eke out a living coaching tennis and boxing, giving English lessons and taking up any writing jobs he was offered. This included collaborating with his friend, Ivan Lukash, on sketches for Berlin's cabaret theatre, as well as scenarios and librettos for opera, ballet and film. He even auditioned for acting roles, and at one time seriously contemplated a career as a movie star. In January 1924 he completed a five-act verse play, *The Tragedy of Mr Morn*, and over the next two years added a further fifteen stories to the half-dozen already either completed or published. By November 1925 he was making final revisions to his first novel, *Mary*.

Mary is rare in Nabokov's fiction in that it contains some of his most explicitly autobiographical writing, including snippets from five of Valentina Shulgin's love letters. On returning to it over 40 years later, he was taken aback by the 'headiness' of its 'personal reality'. Its long, evocative passages of reminiscence reappear in the Tamara chapter (twelve) of his 1967 autobiography, *Speak, Memory*, albeit subtly diminished by the intervening decades, and with some key scenes – 'convalescence, barn concert, boat ride' – forgotten.[49] Initially entitled *Happiness*, just one chapter of the original text appeared as a short story, 'A Letter that Never Reached Russia', published two months before *Mary* in January 1926. The novel was greeted with great praise. The critic Yuly Aikhenval´d hailed Nabokov as 'a new Turgenev',[50] describing his prose as 'suffused with life, with meaning, with psyche'. Nabokov later commented that writing *Mary* constituted the 'careful reconstruction of my artificial but beautiful, beautifully exact Russia'.[51] By putting so much of his own history into his hero's past, Nabokov also saw the novel as a means 'of getting rid of oneself, before going on to better things'.[52]

The story is set in Berlin during a week in April 1924. A motley collection of Russian émigrés, among them Lev Ganin, a young intellectual with an elusive past, Anton Podtyagin, an elderly poet and Aleksey Alfyorov, a middle-aged businessman, share a few

Charlottenburg, under the bridge of the Stadtbahn, 1920s.

cramped rooms in a dingy boarding house alongside the noisy main line of the city's Stadtbahn. The émigrés dream of returning to the old Russia or moving on to a better life but are stalled by overwhelming apathy and stultifying hopelessness. The trains that pass by relentlessly day and night serve as constant reminders of the land they have left, the limbo in which they now exist and the prospect of other possible, glimmering futures that seem so frustratingly unattainable. Both Podtyagin and Ganin are desperate to leave Germany. Podtyagin is prevented merely by the fact that he hasn't the right papers, Ganin by an all-consuming and paralysing spiritual atrophy. One evening, by chance, Ganin discovers that Alfyorov's wife, who is due to join him in Berlin in a matter of days, is his first love, Mary. This throws him into an intense and sustained nostalgic reverie, in which he rapturously and vibrantly relives his affair with her, set against the tantalizing backdrop of a lost Russia. Determined to intercept her on her arrival, Ganin devises a last-minute plan to prevent Alfyorov from meeting her at the railway station, but on his way to confront her, he suddenly changes his mind and boards another train at a different station, bound for France.

The central theme of *Mary* is remembering, made explicit in the epigraph from Pushkin's *Eugene Onegin* which opens the novel: 'Having recalled intrigues of former years, / having recalled a former love.'[53] This is not a casual act but a powerful process whereby the shadows of the past become more real and vital than the tangible present. It is a process that enables Ganin to overcome his sense of loss, not just of his home and his love, but most significantly of himself. Just as he is about to descend to the depths of resigned futility, his consciousness is flooded with memories which obliterate utterly any vestige of his present world, causing a miraculous physical and temporal inversion to take place, whereby the 'robust reality of the past makes a ghost of the present'.[54] That this is more than merely a lapse into self-indulgent escapism is suggested by Ganin's reference to himself as 'a god, re-creating a world that had perished'.[55] This is an act of creation with a defined purpose, not one of simply 'resurrecting' the past but, more importantly, from nothing more than a fleeting image and a distant memory, the palpable form of a precious girl. Remembering has a ritualistic quality, with the potential to bring about the physical manifestation of things that once seemed forever lost to the ravages of time. There are characters throughout Nabokov's fiction who attempt to manipulate the forces of memory in this way, from Ganin and Chorb (in 'The Return of Chorb'), to *Lolita*'s Humbert Humbert and Hugh Person in *Transparent Things*, and yet they are often exposed as deeply misguided, tragic figures pursuing fruitless quests for impossible dreams. That Ganin should abandon his reunion with Mary seems, initially, to make no sense and yet, by changing his plans at the last minute, he concedes to its essential irrelevance to his current predicament. This Nabokov renders through a key change in perspective which initiates a parallel space/time reversal. As he leaves to meet Mary, Ganin is struck by the early morning cast of the city streets which seems to share the same radiant brilliance of his recollections. The potency of this vision causes the vague, insubstantial world of his Berlin, the émigrés and their boarding house, to be instantly and irretrievably consigned to the shadows of the past, and with them, Russia and Mary. Finally free, Ganin turns his focus to a new, urgent present, and the exciting prospect of an unknown future.

Nabokov's imperative of 'getting rid of oneself' is mirrored by the transformation Ganin undergoes at the end of the novel. This is compounded by the extent to which Ganin's character can be identified with the tradition of the 'superfluous man' in Russian literature. Classic traits of apathy, alienation, boredom, frustration, amorality, cold detachment, cynicism and disenchantment, set against a history of romantic and daring exploits undercut by present inertia, would have made Ganin instantly recognizable to a contemporary émigré audience and qualified him as a truly Russian hero, in the mould of Lermontov's Pechorin or Pushkin's Onegin. It is interesting that Nabokov should have made his first major fictional protagonist so unequivocally Russian but then boldly peopled his next novel with an entirely German cast. It is as if he deliberately poured all these qualities into Ganin in order that he could leave him, along with the 'destitution', 'nostalgia' and 'human humidity' of his world, behind.[56]

For Nabokov, this process of 'getting rid of oneself' was not simply a means of releasing his art from the shackles of a personal past, but of disengaging from the stifling encumbrance of shared nostalgia. Through Ganin, Nabokov demonstrates new ways of perceiving the world such that memory no longer acts as a negative, entropic force, but rather one of liberation and inspiration.

In 'The Word', Nabokov's narrator struggles to articulate his grief, to describe adequately his beloved Russia, to express the enormity of his loss, to free himself from sorrow, but he cannot communicate 'the most important thing'.[57] In *Mary*, Nabokov suggests that this 'most important thing' no longer matters, that there are other ways to relinquish suffering and regain a sense of bliss, not by resurrecting past happiness but, as Ganin demonstrates, by refocusing on the objective present, to realize the potential for joy in the most mundane details of everyday life.

This emphasis on altered perspectives is reiterated throughout Nabokov's early work. In 'A Letter that Never Reached Russia' the narrator refers to his happiness as 'a kind of challenge' that counteracts his loneliness, a force that will remain, contained in all the things that brought him such joy – 'in the moist reflection of a streetlamp, in the cautious bend of stone steps that descend into the canal's black waters, in the smiles of a dancing couple'. Similarly, in the 1924 story, 'Beneficence', the narrator derives inordinate pleasure from the sound of wet branches glancing against the roof of a streetcar:

> The tram would chime and start, the gleam of the streetlamps shattered in the wet glass, and, with a sensation of poignant happiness, I awaited the repetition of those meek, lofty sounds.[58]

Meanwhile, despite the unrelenting disasters that plague the life of Morn, the hero of Nabokov's 1924 play, he maintains his sense of the miraculous and, even when all else seems hopeless, is able to rediscover true happiness.[59]

At the same time, this ability to marvel at the mundane world – 'to wonder at trifles'[60] – is key to overcoming the pain of loss and mortality's arbitrary and chaotic destructive power. The 1923 story, 'Gods', echoes the notion of a life-force being released after death contained in the verses Nabokov wrote for his father only a year before. Whilst his father's spirit is contained in the waters of a brook, here the spirit of a couple's dead child can be sensed everywhere and in everything. The father's narrative, or 'fable' as he calls it, is for his dead son, whom he is convinced can hear him because 'words', he believes, 'have no borders'. He cannot and will not share his wife's sorrow, for he senses the presence of his child in the abundance of objects that surround him. His perspective could be interpreted as sentimental indulgence or, simply, dissociative denial, if it weren't for the fact that his vision is utterly non-discriminatory, embracing everything from the glow of light-bulb filaments on an underground train to a patch of 'wan' rubbish-strewn grass. The strange beauty of these arbitrary things persuades him that 'there is no death', that 'there can be no death', but more so, that contained in them is an eternal, universal, life-affirming energy. 'You and I shall have a new, golden son', he declares, 'a creation of your tears and my fables. Today I understood the beauty of intersecting wires in the sky, and the hazy mosaic of factory chimneys, and this rusty tin with its inside-out, semi-detached, serrated lid.'[61]

A fundamental change in attitude can be wrought, therefore, by the subtlest shift in perspective, enabled by an acute sensitivity to combinations of details, much like the poet's 'manifold awareness' which generates a vaunted, inviolable objectivity. This is particularly evident in the 'avid, sharp-eyed' narrative of the 1925 story, 'The Fight'. As two men confront each other in the street, Nabokov's narrator watches with cool dispassion, 'enthralled' by the 'reflections of the streetlamp on the distorted faces, the strained sinew in Krause's naked neck'.[62] As Krause knocks his adversary to the ground, the narrator is left to consider the aftermath. He wonders whether he should perhaps have presented events differently, focused more on the human dimension, on the suffering inflicted, demonstrated greater empathy and compassion. Ultimately, however, he defends the poet's perspective:

what matters is not the human pain or joy at all but, rather, the play of shadow and light on a live body, the harmony of trifles assembled on this particular day, at this particular moment, in a unique and inimitable way.[63]

Whilst this stance distinctly echoes Bergson's privileging of an artistic vision, whereby 'man glimpses reality through the film of familiarity and conventionality that obscures it',[64] it also deploys the Russian Formalist process of *ostranenie*, or 'making strange', whereby art serves to reveal the aesthetic and hyper-real qualities of ordinary objects by disrupting habitual modes of visualization and confounding perceptual expectations.[65] Nabokov's emphasis on 'making strange' is also suggestive of the presence of 'other' worlds, or an 'anterior reality', reminiscent of the Russian Symbolist impulse, which sought to reveal a transcendent essence that lay beyond 'the concrete presence of an object'.[66] Nabokov's combination of these elements in his early work defines the unique quality of his descriptive style. In 'The Razor' (1926), for example, an everyday street scene is transformed into something lithe and fluid, the focus directed not at the passers-by but at the course of their shadows:

People flashed past, accompanied by their blue shadows, which broke over the edge of the sidewalk and glided fearlessly underneath the glittering wheels of cars that left ribbonlike imprints on the heat-softened asphalt.[67]

By the mid-1920s Nabokov was exploring the consequences for key themes of memory, mortality and the imagination of an acutely objective, altered perspective through a skilful manipulation of plot, imagery, narrative structure and characterization. He was to test and extend these elements over the next decade in an extraordinary range of diverse scenarios, such that they became integral to the very substance of his art.

2

Sirin, Part One:
'Terror' to *The Eye*

The best part of a writer's biography is not the record of his adventures but the story of his style.[1]

In the autumn of 1926, the Nabokovs rented two rooms at 12 Passauer Strasse, where they were to stay for the next two years. Although this was one of many moves during their time in Berlin, they always remained in the same part of the city, the newly absorbed district of Charlottenburg. Centred around the Kurfürstendamm, the area was famous for its cosmopolitan nightlife, developing, since the turn of the century, into a vibrant, decadent centre for innovation and experiment in all things. Attracting writers and artists (Bertolt Brecht, Stefan Zweig, George Grosz, Otto Dix), actors, singers, dancers, musicians and composers (Marlene Dietrich, Peter Lorre, Lotte Lenya, Josephine Baker, Kurt Weill, Arnold Schönberg), theatre and film directors (Erwin Piscator, Max Reinhardt, F. W. Murnau, Robert Wiene, Fritz Lang), Berlin's 'New West' became the driving force behind the city's extraordinary cultural boom of the 1920s. Its explosive energy both complemented and reflected a prevailing and urgent desire for change, expressed through an increasingly volatile social and political scene, fuelled initially by ruinous inflation and then, in 1929, by financial meltdown following the Wall Street Crash. The political turbulence that had dogged Germany in the immediate post-First World War years resurfaced, with fascists, communists and the police clashing violently on Berlin's streets. Unemployment sky-rocketed as the economy began to collapse. By the early 1930s, Germany's institutions of democracy were so undermined that Hitler's National Socialists, who only a few years before had barely made any political impact, faced the real possibility of absolute power.

The Nabokovs were to a great extent isolated and protected from these upheavals by the Russian émigré community. Charlottenburg was very much 'Russian' Berlin, with its Russian bookshops, cafes, bars, restaurants and theatres, including the most famous cabaret, Der Blaue Vogel (The Bluebird) on Goltzstrasse, where the sketches Nabokov wrote with his friend Ivan Lukash were performed. Prominent figures from the Russian arts had either settled in the city or were constantly passing through: writers and poets – Boris Pasternak, Maxim Gorky, Ivan Bunin, Ilya Ehrenburg, Vladimir Mayakovsky, Lev Shestov and Viktor Shklovsky; theatre directors and filmmakers – Konstantin Stanislavsky, Vsevolod Meyerhol´d, Sergey Eisenstein; artists, singers, dancers and musicians – Marc Chagall, Vasily Kandinsky, Fyodor Chaliapin, Anna Pavlova, Vladimir Horowitz and Gregor Piatigorsky. Andrey Bely, on visiting Charlottenburg in the early 1920s, described it as a 'hothouse of yesterday's Russian culture':

> In this part of Berlin you meet people you have not met for years, not to mention your acquaintances; you meet all of Moscow and all of Piter [St Petersburg], Russian Paris, Prague, even Sofia and Belgrade; . . . and if it happens you hear German spoken, you are perplexed: How's that? Germans? What business do they have in 'our' city?[2]

The house on Passauer Strasse overlooked a Russian restaurant and the side entrance to the city's largest department store, the Kaufhaus des Westens. Just a few doors down Nabokov could often be found browsing the vast collection of Russian books at

the Buchhandlung und Leihbibliothek des Westens.[3] Every other
week, in various cafés and apartments, he would attend meetings
of a literary circle founded by Yuly Aikenval´d and Raisa Tatarinov
to read and discuss new writing, which included the work of the
Soviets – Zamyatin, Pilnyak, Olesha, Gladkov and Zoshchenko.
He also made regular appearances at literary readings and charity
balls organized by the Union of Russian Writers and Journalists.
Despite being city-bound, he was even able to pursue, if only vic-
ariously, his lepidopteral interests. In the spring of 1926 he began
visiting a scientist at the Entomological Institute at Dahlem, a
Russian named Moltrecht, 'who spoke so wonderfully, so touch-
ingly, so romantically, about butterflies'. His own successes as a
hunter were minimal, amounting to the apprehension of a solitary moth, albeit a very rare one, which he spotted on a tree trunk
near Charlottenburg's railway station.[4] He also had the chance to
indulge his other great passion – chess – taking on two masters in
an open tournament, one of whom he kept in play for over four
hours. By the autumn he was working on a new play commission,
The Man from the USSR, for the Group Theatre Company, which
was staged the following April. He would write at night, and in
the daytime review poetry for *Rul´*, give lessons in English and
French and coach tennis, whilst Véra took on work as a translator
and typist. 1926, he would later say, was 'one of the happiest years
of my life'.[5]

Nevertheless, the Nabokovs thought Berlin 'a miserable dead
end'. Vladimir complained to Véra that 'hearing German made
him sick'.[6] Although he began to make plans to leave Germany in
late 1932, they stayed, even after Hitler passed his first anti-Jewish
laws the following year, making Véra a potential target for persecution, and after the birth of their son, Dmitri, in 1934. The situation
in Germany 'disgusted' them, but they saw little difference between
this new regime and the Soviet one they had left behind. Like many
other émigrés, Nabokov was 'absolutely sure' that 'sometime in the

Cartoon by S. A.
Tsivinsky in *Segodnya*
(*Today*), August 1924.

next decade we would all be back in a hospitable, remorseful, race-mosa-filled Russia'.[7]

Nabokov once commented that he 'travel[led] through life in a space helmet'.[8] The security he found in his work, his personal life and the extended Russian community enabled him to exist at one remove from the concerns of the wider world. Like his fellow émigrés, he felt he was living in an 'illusory' city, 'among perfectly unimportant strangers' who seemed 'as flat and transparent as figures cut out of cellophane'. These transparent figures were still, however, capable of inflicting 'awful convulsions' that served as stark reminders of 'who was the discarnate captive and who the true lord'.[9]

These 'awful convulsions' notwithstanding, existing on the margins of a 'spectral world' suited Nabokov extremely well. The enforced detachment he experienced as a foreigner in an alien land was to him a bonus, for 'isolation' meant 'liberty and discovery'.[10] Since Germany, its people and its culture held no appeal, it posed no threat to Nabokov's closely guarded autonomy. He refused to improve the 'smattering' of German he had 'picked up' during a six-month stay in Berlin with Sergey in 1910,[11] or learnt subsequently at school, and avoided German books and newspapers. At the same time, the Russian émigré community was so self-sufficient that he could happily disconnect himself from German daily life without compunction.

This sense of abiding and distilled dissociation curiously complemented Nabokov's preoccupation with the mutability of perception and identity that he had already begun to explore in his work. 1926 marked a major development in his elaboration of these themes with the short story 'Terror'. Informed by the psychological and philosophical work of Tolstoy, Shevstov, Pascal, Kant and William James,[12] it presents a scenario of pure and abject panic in the form of a pre-Sartrean existential crisis. The story is narrated by a young poet who describes a series of episodes in which he experiences, initially, a fleeting sense of total estrangement whereby he becomes 'disacquainted' with himself,[13] then an overwhelming night-time horror of death and, finally, an inexplicable, irrational terror at the proximal presence of another human being. This culminates in a complete mental breakdown, following four sleepless nights:

Insomnia had left me with an exceptionally receptive void within my mind. My head seemed made of glass, and the slight cramp in my calves had also a vitreous character . . . My line of communication with the world snapped, I was on my own and the world was on its own, and that world was devoid of sense.[14]

This disacquaintedness is magnified to such an extent that the true reality of the world is suddenly exposed to him 'in all its terrifying nakedness and terrifying absurdity' – 'I was no longer a man, but a naked eye, an aimless gaze moving in an absurd world.' The poet is abruptly saved from descent into total insanity by the death of his lover. Shock and grief obliterate, for a while, all thoughts of 'being and nonbeing', but the poet knows that the intensity of his emotions and his memories of her will fade, and he will have to face again his 'helpless fear of existing', and that this time 'there will be no salvation'.[15]

'Terror' was written to fulfil an aborted commission from the Paris-based émigré journal *Sovremennye zapiski* (*Contemporary Annals*). It is significant for two reasons. Published in January 1927, it brought Nabokov's work for the first time to a wider European audience. Secondly, it marks a discreet but major turning point in Nabokov's fiction, establishing themes and preoccupations that were to become pivotal in his work, concerns he would revisit continually over the next half century.

Deploying the Formalist principle of *ostranenie*, the story wrestles with two of humankind's keenest and most perplexing problems – madness and death. In the 1923 verse drama, *Death*, Nabokov suggests that death holds the prospect of either 'an astonishment' or 'nothing at all'.[16] This is reiterated by Adam Krug in the 1947 novel *Bend Sinister*, who postulates that death is 'either the instantaneous gaining of perfect knowledge' or 'absolute nothingness, *nichto*'.[17] In 'Terror', Nabokov's protagonist argues that

we find comfort in telling ourselves that the world could not exist without us, that it exists only inasmuch as we ourselves exist, inasmuch as we can represent it to ourselves. Death, infinite space, galaxies, all this is frightening, exactly because it transcends the limits of our perception.[18]

By challenging the 'limits of his perception' and confronting the things that terrify him, Nabokov's poet risks his sanity, and yet there is still no prospect of a resolution to his dilemma. The only hope he is given is in the form of his love for another, but this proves to be transitory and vulnerable to the forces of destruction. Nevertheless, the story 'is Nabokov's first attempt in fiction to postulate the role of love as a stabilizing point of reference and defense against cosmic horror, the defamiliarized world-as-it-is'.[19] At the same time, it introduces a dynamic of perpetual vacillation that recurs throughout Nabokov's work between two possible after-death scenarios. Whilst it may be that 'our existence is but a brief crack of light between two eternities of darkness',[20] Nabokov's elaboration of 'other worlds' in his fiction undermines the concept of human life as finite. At the same time, this ability to apprehend the 'shadows linking our state of existence to those other states and modes which we dimly apprehend in our rare moments of irrational perception'[21] is inextricably linked to creativity. This Nabokov made explicit in one of the first lectures he gave after arriving in the United States in 1940:

> That human life is but a first instalment of the serial soul, and that one's individual secret is not lost in the process of earthly dissolution, becomes something more than an optimistic conjecture, and even more than a matter of religious faith, when we remember that only commonsense rules immortality out. A creative writer . . . cannot help feeling that in rejecting the world of the matter-of-fact, in his taking sides with the irrational, the illogical, the inexplicable and the fundamentally good, he is performing something similar in a rudimentary way to what the spirit may be expected to perform, when the time comes, on a vaster and more satisfactory scale.[22]

Whilst grief saves the narrator of 'Terror' (if only temporarily) from madness, elsewhere it threatens to destroy its victims . In two earlier stories, 'The Return of Chorb' (1925) and 'Wingstroke' (1923), both protagonists suffer the sudden and brutal loss of their wives – Chorb by accidental electrocution, Kern by suicide. Each man turns to an extreme means of dispelling grief – Kern by deciding to shoot himself, Chorb by attempting to replace his dead wife with an 'immortal' image, constructed from the revisited details of their brief honeymoon. This process of partial resurrection, however, proves to be both tragic and comical, for Chorb's efforts bring about a near transmigration of his wife's soul into the body of a prostitute he pays to sleep beside him in their wedding-night bed. Ironically, his mission backfires. Waking in the night he turns to the prostitute lying next to him, believing her to be his dead wife, resurrected. He starts to scream, 'horribly, with a visceral force', emitting 'a ghastly deep-drawn howl'. The shock jolts him out of his grief-stricken state, releasing him, finally, and bathetically, from his 'ordeal'.[23]

Kern, on the other hand, has lost his wife after seven years of 'ecstatic love'. Her death has exposed an 'abyss' of infinite nothingness that 'breathes and sucks everything in' and his happiness with her is reduced to yet another 'scrap' in a 'shaky row of varicoloured screens with which he shielded himself from cosmic drafts' – 'they billowed, these scraps, with the wind outside, tore, fell one by one.' The loss of this last scrap has weakened his ability to 'escape from the unknown, from the vertiginous sky'. After six months of 'dull melancholy', he ventures to a ski resort at Zermatt, but its 'tipsy', 'lighthearted' atmosphere offers little in the way of distraction or protection. There he meets a young Englishwoman, Isabel, but Kern still resigns himself, with relief, to self-destruction – 'And death seemed to him like a gliding dream, a fluffy fall. No thoughts, no palpitations, no aches.'[24] However, in deciding to submit himself to the 'abyss' he inadvertently releases the supernatural forces that he senses pressing ever closer against the flimsy barriers of his world, and they emerge in the form of a fallen angel. Once again the imagined or intended consequences of deliberate action turn out to be highly unpredictable, for it is not Kern whom the angel seeks out, but Isabel. Inspired by the demon of Lermontov's classic poem, Nabokov's angel seduces Isabel and when he suspects her betrayal, destroys her, on the very day that Kern plans to commit suicide.[25]

Nabokov's evocation of the supernatural in his early fiction extends to another story, 'Natasha', written in 1924. Khrenov, Natasha's father, is fatally ill. His young daughter – the only member of his family to have survived into emigration – is caring for him in a small Berlin apartment. Tending to his every need, she is exhausted but undaunted. It is as if she is guarding a secret, something that protects her from sorrow. She confesses to their neighbour that she has visions, but then dismisses them as fantasy. Nevertheless, her clairvoyance is confirmed at the end of the story when she sees and talks to her father in the street, unaware that he is already dead. This vision is directly preceded by a sensation of lightness and heat, reminiscent of the deliria Nabokov suffered as a child:

> Natasha seemed propelled by sails, as if her fatigue sustained her, endowed her with wings and made her weightless. . . . She felt that she was growing weak, that hot, silent billows were coursing along her spine.[26]

Natasha associates this airy, dream-like feeling with fatigue, but it in fact signals a state of being which grants her access to another realm – the realm of the dead which, unlike Kern's abyss, is benign and free of fear. Khrenov's ghost is smiling and kind, gentle and unthreatening, utterly distinct from the terrifying prospect of Chorb's resurrected wife.

From the explicit manifestation of ghosts, demons and resurrected spirits in his early stories, to the more discreet yet no less palpable presence of 'otherworldly' elements in his late fiction, Nabokov's treatment of the supernatural is central to the elaboration of themes of death and the hereafter across his work. That this was, in fact, his 'main theme' was confirmed by Véra Nabokov in her foreword to her husband's posthumously published 1979 collection of Russian poetry. *Potustoronnost´* – the beyond, the hereafter, the other side – she claimed, 'saturates everything he wrote'.[27] Nabokov first discussed this term in a 1922 essay on Rupert Brooke, in which he stated that 'not a single poet has looked into the twilight of the hereafter [*potustoronnosti*] with such tormented and creative penetration'.[28] The essay refers to elements of Brooke's poetry that can be identified as the intensely expressive emblems which Nabokov deployed to signal the presence of 'other worlds' in his fiction ('tenderness, forest shadows, transparent streams'), whilst Brooke's assertion that death is 'only an astonishment, a surprise', pre-empts the exact same contention voiced in Nabokov's 1923 play, *Death*.[29]

Although influenced by his own clairvoyant experiences and his mother's 'sixth' sense, Nabokov's metaphysical thinking was also informed by a tradition in Russian literature, from Lermontov and Gogol to Tolstoy, Dostoevsky and Blok, that foregrounded fantasy and the supernatural, compounded by a cultural fascination with the paranormal which reached its zenith at the turn of the twentieth century. At the same time, Nabokov's exposure to the work of Edgar Allan Poe and H. G. Wells as a boy and, subsequently, Brooke, Walter de la Mare and Lewis Carroll in early adulthood, reinforced and extended his curiosity regarding the possibilities of transcendence through art and the existence of alternate temporal and spatial dimensions. 'Much of De la Mare's quietly fantastic poetry and prose', for example, 'strongly hints that our world merely masks a deeper reality', applying 'the name "the otherworld" to this higher reality in at least one of his works.'[30] At the same time, the 'imperceptible influence of "dear ghosts" is almost imperceptibly but deliberately and persistently displayed in a great number of De La Mare's stories'.[31] This sense of an 'invisible world of intangible presences'[32] coincides with the fantastic, nonsensical parallel universe of Lewis Carroll's *Alice in Wonderland*. Of all Carroll's mundane access points to Wonderland – the rabbit hole, the garden door, the looking-glass – it was the potential of the mirror, and indeed any reflective surface, to disclose unexpected vistas that most captured Nabokov's imagination. Just as he published his Russian version of *Alice*, he was working on a story, 'Sounds', in which the familiar reflection of the sky in water is transformed, by a simple shift in perspective, into a fleeting prospect of some inverse, nether world – 'puddles looked like holes in the sand, apertures onto some other heavens that were gliding past underground.'[33]

If in 'Terror' love serves as a stabilizing force against 'cosmic horror', in 'Natasha' it lifts the mask of 'our world' to reveal the 'deeper reality' that lies behind it, a dimension peopled by the spirits of the dead. As Natasha's love for her father exposes a life after death, so in another 1924 story, 'Christmas', the very force of a man's love for his son initiates a sequence of mundane acts which form a discreet but meaningful commemoration, bringing about a miraculous release.

It is Christmas Eve and Slepstov has returned to his country home to bury his young son. Wandering around the cold, empty, snow-bound house he comes across his son's things – his butterfly collection, a notebook, a butterfly net and an old biscuit tin containing a dry, brown, 'exotic' cocoon. Slepstov takes these few precious objects back to his quarters, but overcome with grief and suddenly confronted with a future that is 'bared and comprehensible', 'ghastly in its sadness, humiliatingly pointless, sterile' and 'devoid of miracles', he decides to kill himself. Meanwhile,

his modest act of remembrance triggers an unforeseen process –
in the warmth of Slepstov's room the cocoon in the biscuit tin
hatches and a 'great Attacus moth' emerges. The creature is the
'great Oriental moth' his son had been muttering about in his
delirium only a few days before,[34] and is thus directly associated
with the boy's death as an emblem of transformation, transcendence and immortality. Throughout Nabokov's fiction, moths and
butterflies represent 'grace and beauty and art at their highest',[35]
possessing a divine, otherworldly quality. They are the vessels that
transport the souls of the dead, 'wild angels'[36] that exist in all realms
of being – free, joyful and rapturous – and are a consistent, abiding
force of 'tender, ravishing, almost human happiness'.[37]

In his introduction to the story's English translation, Nabokov
describes it as 'oddly resembl[ing] the type of chess problem
called "selfmate"'.[38] In a series of minimal moves, by gathering
his son's belongings, by demonstrating his love through acts
of remembrance and preservation and thus initiating, albeit
inadvertently, a miraculous, life-affirming metamorphosis,
Slepstov 'checkmates his own despair'.[39] This was the first time
Nabokov deployed chess as a structural and thematic device. He
was to redeploy it, some six years later, in *The Defense*, with far
bleaker consequences.

In the summer of 1927, the Nabokovs chaperoned three boys
on a holiday to the picturesque Baltic seaside resort at Binz. There,
Nabokov came up with the idea for his next novel, *King, Queen,
Knave*, which culminates in a conspiracy to commit murder by
engineering a drowning accident. Coincidentally, Nabokov had
only recently read and discussed a new American novel with one of
his students – Theodore Dreiser's *An American Tragedy* – which also
features a 'murder disguised as an accidental drowning'. Although
the scenarios may be similar, *King, Queen, Knave* rejects the 'relentless' determinism of Dreiser's murder/tragedy, replacing it instead
with a powerful dynamic of unpredictability, injecting an element

of 'caprice' which subverts the reader's expectations and redirects the course of the story's dénouement.[40]

King, Queen, Knave was to initiate a process of 'gradual inner disentanglement' which offered Nabokov the 'fairytale freedom' and complete lack of emotional involvement in his subject that 'answered [his] dream of pure invention'. As he was later to comment, 'expatriation, destitution, nostalgia had no effect on its elaborate and rapturous composition'. Like *Mary*, the novel is set in contemporary Berlin, but deliberately moves away from the familiar milieu of Russian émigré society to focus on the modern Berliner. The story's protagonists are a 'set of exclusively German characters':[41] Kurt Dreyer, an affluent and successful, middle-aged, middle-class businessman, his 34-year-old wife, Martha – glamorous, materialistic and socially aspirant – and Dreyer's young nephew, Franz, who becomes Martha's lover and co-conspirator.

King, Queen, Knave is darkly comic, and its protagonists unremittingly and unredeemably despicable. Much of the novel's comedy is generated by dramatic irony, by Franz's farcical ineptitude and the grotesque and repugnant physicality of the protagonists' daily lives, which persistently rises from beneath a thin veneer of respectability. Key to the elaboration of banality in the novel is the dynamic of *poshlost* – a term Nabokov chose to denote 'the obviously trashy', the 'falsely important, the falsely beautiful, the falsely clever, the falsely attractive',[42] which was 'not only an esthetic judgment but also a moral indictment'.[43] Introduced here for the first time, it is embodied, most starkly and calamitously, by Martha Dreyer's bourgeois pretensions.

Meanwhile, another major theme, fate, emerges as a dominant force. By proceeding with her murderous schemes, Martha subjects herself to the vagaries of fate, something which severely disrupts her instinctive compulsion to control her world. 'Life should proceed according to plan', she asserts, 'straight and strict, without freakish twists and wiggles'.[44] That the narrative is replete with 'twists and wiggles' – near escapes, near collisions, chance meetings, near misses – undermines her rigid stance, and yet she is ready to embrace any occurrence which she can interpret as supporting Dreyer's demise and her idyllic future with Franz.

Central to the novel's ironic dynamic is the theme of literal and metaphorical blindness, most overtly depicted by Franz, who is not only virtually blind without his spectacles, but also rendered utterly blind by Martha's seductive influence – 'His eyes were totally submissive behind their well-wiped lenses.' Dreyer sees a potential murderer in every passing stranger but never suspects the people closest to him, whilst Martha is so blinded by lust and greed that she forgets about the risks to herself. She is also oblivious to the latent evil in Franz, which inevitably emerges once he is free of her clutches and the reader is given a chilling glimpse of his future incarnation 'as a very old and very sick man, guilty of worse sins than avunculicide'.[45]

Whilst in *Mary*, altered perception initiates a process of revelation and release, here Nabokov combines this with temporal and spatial shifts to assert his authority over the scenario, to emphasize the degree to which his protagonists are trapped within it – like 'galley slaves'[46] entirely subject to his will – and to expose the inherent artifice of the novel's world. This is established in the very opening sequence, as a train pulls out of a station. The 'resilient jolt' of the station clock's minute-hand 'sets a whole world in motion', and the forward movement of the train becomes a metaphor for the inexorable progress of Nabokov's story which, unlike the train, has no obvious, predetermined destination. Deploying once again the principle of *ostranenie*, Nabokov adopts a literal visual perspective that sustains the briefly unsettling but familiar sensation of motion seemingly transferred from a moveable object to an immovable environment, a sensation that reason and logic would normally quickly dispel:

one by one the pillars will start walking past, carrying off on an unknown journey cigarette butts, used tickets, flecks of sunlight and spittle; a luggage handcart will glide by, its wheels motionless; it will be followed by a news stall hung with seductive magazine covers . . . and people, people, people on the moving platform, themselves moving their feet, yet standing still, striding forward, yet retreating as in an agonizing dream full of incredible effort.[47]

This fantastic prospect introduces a disruptive dynamic, a sense of things not being quite what they seem, and asserts the importance of the unexpected and the folly of a presumed reliance on conventional modes of apprehension. From the outset, it is a theme that undercuts the entirety of the narrative, existing discreetly behind the facade of the novel's foregrounded action. For example, when Franz wakes up on his first morning in Berlin, he experiences the sensation of rising through layers of consciousness, arriving at 'new moments of specious awareness' that turn out to be further dimensions of his dream-state. What seems to be reality 'abruptly loses the tingle and tang of reality' such that true reality becomes impossible to determine – 'Yet who knows? Is this reality, *the* final reality, or just a new deceptive dream?'

This sense of uncertainty, of existing in a fabulous fantasy, is compounded by the fact that Franz must spend his first day in Berlin without his glasses, which he had stepped on the night before, and try to navigate the city in a myopic haze. A world that would otherwise seem categorically absolute becomes unnervingly yet exquisitely incorporeal, 'delicate', 'weightless', 'radiant and unstable', an ethereal realm of mirages, fog and shadows.[48] Meanwhile, the novel's illusory quality is further magnified by the lurking presence of Franz's landlord and former magician, 'old' Enricht, who believes – in a kind of jaundiced parody of Nabokov's role as omniscient author – that he has 'created Franz with a few deft dabs of his facile fancy':

Berlin at night, 1928.

For he knew perfectly well . . . that the whole world was but a trick of his, and that all those people . . . owed their existence to the power of his imagination and suggestion and the dexterity of his hands.[49]

Although on one level, *King, Queen, Knave* is a straightforward story of corruption, lust and murder, in many respects it initiates the structural and thematic complexity of Nabokov's subsequent work. Apart from introducing the destructive, three-way relationships that were to dominate *Laughter in the Dark*, *Lolita* and *Ada*, with its narrative strategies demonstrably on display it provides a useful means of identifying the crucial elements of Nabokov's future 'constructions'.[50]

Nevertheless, the novel had a mixed reception. 'While Russian émigré critics . . . disagreed about the merits of Nabokov's work, many of them did agree on one point: they kept referring to his "un-Russianness," to his lack of ties with Russian literature and its traditions.'[51] He was even accused of having 'meticulously copied from mediocre German models'.[52] However, these critics overlooked the ways in which Nabokov's work was very much embedded in the Russian tradition. His artistic philosophy had its closest affinities with the three dominant principles of the Symbolist movement of late Imperial Russia – its emphasis on individualism and 'the role of the artist in indicating a higher reality beyond the sensual world'.[53] Nabokov's famous and very public defence of his creative autonomy in later life reverberates with statements made by leading figures of the Silver Age. The Polish writer Stanislaw Przybyszewski argued that 'the artist is neither a servant nor a guide, does not belong to the people or to the world, does not serve any idea or any society', whilst Sergey Diaghilev contended that 'the great strength of art lies precisely in the fact that it is self-sufficient, self-purposeful, and, above all, free'.[54] Nabokov's gamesmanship, his stance as a 'plotter' of complex fictive puzzles, can be located in Bely's contention that 'every novel is a game of hide and seek with the reader',[55] and that only by pursuing the writer's clues in the correct way can the reader discover his 'spectacular secret'.[56] At the same time, 'the conscious "literariness" of Acmeism, and its values of self-discipline and craftsmanship',[57] along with its 'celebration' of 'perceptual acuity'[58] echo Nabokov's championing of a meticulous attention to detail and a precision of purpose and method – 'In high art and pure science detail is everything', he argued.[59] All these elements he was to combine in his third novel, the tragic tale of a chess grandmaster, driven to self-destruction by the force of his obsession for the game.

In November 1928, two months after its publication, the German publisher Ullstein bought the rights for *King, Queen, Knave* for 7,300 marks, three times the sum paid for *Mary*. This meant that the Nabokovs could take a break, and in February 1929 they set off for the Pyrenees where, for the first time in a decade, Nabokov was able to hunt butterflies. He also began work on his new novel, *The Defense*, writing at a small desk 'covered by a checked tablecloth', with an 'overful ashtray' and 'four volumes of Dahl's [Russian]

Nabokov writing
The Defense,
February 1929.

dictionary stacked against the wall'.[60] Returning to Berlin in June
with a 'wonderful' butterfly hoard and the Ullstein money not yet
exhausted, the Nabokovs bought a plot of land south of Berlin
where they hoped to build a new home. They stayed there over the
summer, but the building project never materialized. In the meantime, Nabokov was busy writing, and preparing his first collection
of stories, *The Return of Chorb*, which was published the following
year. By August he was approaching the 'last full stop' of his new
novel – 'a complicated, complicated thing' with 'monstrously
difficult themes'.[61]

Nabokov's 'monstrously difficult themes' encompass social,
emotional and psychological dysfunction – alienation, isolation,

estrangement, entrapment, obsession, delusion and madness. The strange genius of Nabokov's weirdly lovable, 'virtually inert hero'[62] is driven by a fear of engagement with the physical world. Chess offers a sanctuary, a realm ruled by the intellect and the imagination that transcends the oppressive confines of materiality. As it has in previous works, love also offers, if only briefly, the prospect of protection, but Luzhin's passion for the game is ultimately more powerful, and it is chess that remains his primary 'defense', even though it is the game itself that poses the greatest threat to his corporeal being, and his sanity. The 'exact and relentlessly unfolding' patterns that comprise Luzhin's world he at first interprets as benevolent signs of a preordained fate, but these patterns ultimately turn against him, close in on him and ensnare him in an endless, reductive cycle. Ultimately, Luzhin is faced with no other choice but to escape 'the trap', the 'evil lure' of the chessboard, and to literally "'drop out of the game"'[63] by throwing himself to his death from a fifth-storey window.[64]

Luzhin's death plunge prefigures a series of attempts by the heroes of Nabokov's fiction to literally step out of and into another world (Martin Edelweiss in *Glory*, Cincinnatus C. in *Invitation to a Beheading*, Hugh Person in *Transparent Things*). Within the novel itself it neatly closes another regressive cycle, initiated by Luzhin's crawling through a window as a young boy at his parents' country house in a futile attempt to avoid being sent to school. Throughout Nabokov's work, windows offer the prospect of access to 'other' worlds, whilst the vertiginous pull of gravity is a powerful force to which many of his protagonists are drawn. Luzhin surrenders to gravity as he breaks down, and is comically mistaken for a drunk. The scene recalls the slapstick antics of 1920s silent movie comedians – Charlie Chaplin, Harold Lloyd and Buster Keaton – all of whom Nabokov cited as favourites,[65] and inspired the 'commercial sketches', or 'Locomotions' he wrote for the Bluebird club.[66] The novel's 'monstrous theme' of chess serves as a metaphor for the identifiably Gnostic entrapment Luzhin suffers. His conflict is with the material world, and yet chess offers him only temporary liberation, a transient relief at the highest cost to his physical and mental well-being. At the same time, the Gnostic dimension of Luzhin's experience suggests that his dilemma is governed by something other than simply his chess-dominated pathology, that there are more discreet, elusive forces at work implying, perhaps, that his paranoia is not entirely unfounded.

Throughout his career, Nabokov consistently and stubbornly refused to declare allegiance to any form of organized religion, making such evasive statements as 'I know more than I can express in words, and the little I can express would not have been expressed, had I not known more.'[67] Nevertheless, his metaphysics of transcendence incorporate identifiable elements of Christianity – a heavenly divinity, angels, devils, even a God – combined with the supernatural, mystic spiritualism and Gnosticism, namely the belief that 'man is trapped in an evil material world, and that his physical body is the prison of his soul'.[68] This is very much Luzhin's dilemma, made more disturbingly explicit in the subsequent nightmarish worlds of *The Eye* and *Invitation to a Beheading*.

Even before it appeared in book form, serialized in *Sovremennye zapiski* from October 1929, *The Defense* generated 'a contemptibly envious clamor'.[69] On reading the first few chapters, one of the most prominent figures in Russian émigré culture, the writer and critic Nina Berberova, described Nabokov as 'a tremendous, mature, sophisticated modern writer', 'a great Russian writer, like a Phoenix ... born from the fire and ashes of revolution and exile'. Meanwhile, the Nobel Prize-winning author and doyen of Russian émigré letters, Ivan Bunin, conceded that 'this kid has snatched a gun and done away with the whole older generation, myself included'.[70] Critics hailed Nabokov as 'the biggest gift of the emigration to Russian literature', acknowledging his success in 'synthesizing the Russian literary tradition with Western innovations, and in combining [Russia's] concern for psychology and [the West's] fascination with plot and perfection of form'.[71]

Amidst this clamour, Nabokov spent the autumn classifying butterflies in the Dahlem museum, writing reviews and finalizing his first short story collection for publication. Towards the end of the year he began work on a new novella, *The Eye*, completing it in February 1930, when he read the first chapter to a meeting of the Union of Russian Writers at Berlin's Kaffee Schmidt.

With *The Eye*, Nina Berberova argued, 'something fundamentally changed in the calibre of [Nabokov's] works'.[72] In its 'pursuit of an investigation which leads the protagonist through a hell of mirrors and ends in the merging of twin images',[73] it demonstrates Nabokov's most explicit rejection of 'the world of the matter-of-fact', and his deliberate alignment with 'the irrational, the illogical and the inexplicable'.

The story's hero/narrator, Smurov, attempts suicide after suffering the humiliation of being beaten up by his lover's jealous husband. Waking up in a hospital bed he believes that, despite his bandaged gunshot wound, his attempt was a success, and that his world has been transformed into a 'postexistent chimera' in which he exists as an 'onlooker', a free-floating, anonymous, mutable spirit.[74] As Smurov's persona begins to mutate and divide, the identity of the dominant first-person narrative voice becomes uncertain. This uncertainty is compounded by Smurov's dispersal into 'various images of himself fashioned by everyone he encounters',[75] until eventually his sense of self disintegrates entirely:

> For I do not exist: there exist but thousands of mirrors that reflect me. With every acquaintance I make, the population of phantoms resembling me increases. . . . I alone do not exist. . . . a fetus in reverse, my image, too will dwindle and die within that last witness.[76]

In the meantime, reality 'keeps intruding, wreaking havoc with what the "I" thinks to be his imaginary world',[77] whilst Smurov's dissociative state reaches a critical point where even space and time begin to dissolve.

Beyond the story's foregrounded themes of mirroring and doubling exists a rich subtextual patterning of imagery and allusion embedded in seemingly inconsequential details. For example, a covert allusion to a particular species of butterfly complements and extends the implications of multiple perspectives.[78] The process of 'classifying' Smurov's many masks is likened to that of identifying this butterfly, which turns out to be a Scarce Copper – in Russian, *mnogoglazka* ('the many-eyed'), and in French, 'Argus'[79] (in Greek mythology, Argus is transformed into a peacock, and his spies become the eyespots on the bird's tail-feathers). These details resonate with references to peacocks throughout the narrative – Smurov lives at 5 Peacock Street and wears a 'bright blue tie with a peacock sheen'[80] – details that combine to evocatively reinforce his role as a disembodied, solitary observer:

> I have realized that the only happiness in this world is to observe, to spy, to watch, to scrutinize oneself and others, to be nothing but a big, slightly vitreous, somewhat bloodshot, unblinking eye.[81]

There is a fundamental paradox at the heart of *The Eye* for, despite his bizarre schemes and fantasies, its disturbed hero is 'fundamentally good'. This goodness, according to Nabokov, is contained in the 'forces of imagination' which 'remain steadfastly on Smurov's side'.[82] Such sustained paradox and ambivalence denies any prospect of closure and yet, in its celebration of complexity, ambiguity and 'mystery', serves a very specific, revelationary purpose. 'A good reader,' Nabokov argued, 'a major reader, an active and creative reader is a rereader.'[83] Through this process of return the reader begins to engage with the 'nerves' of a text, whereby its 'subliminal coordinates' and 'secret points',[84] its 'interesting shades and underwater patterns'[85] are gradually and spectacularly disclosed.

Smurov's antecedents can be found in Edgar Allan Poe's 'Ligeia' and 'William Wilson', Dostoevsky's *The Double* and Valery Briusov's 'In the Mirror', and also the 1926 German silent feature *The Student of Prague*, starring Conrad Veidt, which Nabokov could well have seen on one of his frequent visits to the cinema during his time in Berlin.[86] The story's 'audacity and originality'[87] is also strongly reminiscent of the unique qualities of Chekhov's fiction. In a rare declaration, Nabokov cited Chekhov as his 'predecessor'.[88] Equally, as writers and professional scientists – Chekhov a doctor, Nabokov a lepidopterist – they both deployed in their art 'the precision of poetry and the excitement of pure science'.[89] Without 'attention to the specific detail, to the unique image', Nabokov argued, 'there can be no art, no genius, no Chehov [*sic*], no terror, no tenderness, and no surprise'.[90] Like Nabokov, Chekhov was averse 'to ready-made devices and stereotypes of every sort'.[91] His protagonists were often dysfunctional, deeply selfish, manipulative and egomaniacal, their grand future plans abandoned or failed, featured in unpredictable, disrupted and inconclusive scenarios. Both writers also suffered extreme and unremittingly negative criticism. Even after the publication of *The Defense*, Nabokov continued to be attacked for his un-Russianness. Like Chekhov, he was accused of undermining the Russian literary tradition, of coldness, emptiness, indifference and artistic aimlessness. Nevertheless, Nabokov remained undeterred, finding 'the disparities' of his critics' judgements 'amusing'.[92] By May 1930 he was writing his next novel, *Glory*.

3

Sirin, Part Two:
Glory to *The Gift*

To be a good visionary you must be a good observer. The better you see
the earth the finer your perception of heaven will be.[1]

By the early 1930s, the Russian population in Berlin had dwindled
to around 30,000. Meanwhile, in France it had grown to nearly
half a million, with Paris now the European centre of the Russian
emigration. In October 1931, *Rul´* was forced to close down, and
Nabokov began publishing stories in the Paris-based journal
Poslednie novosti (*The Latest News*). Over the next decade, *Sovremennye zapiski* would also continue to print his short fiction and,
following the serialization of *The Defense*, all his longer works.
Nevertheless, the Nabokovs were still finding it hard to make ends
meet. Vladimir complained that the 'stupidest worry of my life
has been a fruitless struggle with poverty'.[2] On top of her secretarial job, Véra gave English lessons and worked as a tour guide
for an American travel agency. She continued working even when,
as unemployment soared to seven million, she could be legally
sacked as a second wage-earner, and well after the introduction of
restrictions on Jewish employment. Early in 1932, the Nabokovs
were forced to move from the rooms they had been renting in
Luitpoldstrasse to Westfälische Strasse and then in August to a
'charming, spacious flat'[3] in Nestorstrasse, owned by Véra's cousin,
just off the Kurfürstendamm, where they were to stay for the next
five years.

Nabokov completed his fifth novel, *Glory*, in December 1930. Its purpose, he claimed, was to 'give the brighter side of my life', to stress 'the thrill and the glamour' of 'the most ordinary pleasures' and 'the seemingly meaningless adventures of a lonely life'.[4] He was to call it his 'happiest thing',[5] and identified its main theme as 'the overcoming of fear, the glory and rapture of that victory'.[6] His hero, the 'resplendent' Martin Edelweiss, he cited as one of his 'favourite creatures'.[7] The story follows the dreams and ambitions of a young man searching for romantic fulfilment in 'the bliss of spiritual solitude and the excitement of travel'.[8] Modestly thwarted at every turn, unable to emulate the achievements of his peers, he decides to pursue a secret, 'audacious' and perilous exploit,[9] to surreptitiously cross an invisible border into an 'unknown land' – Soviet Russia. Martin is a 'rarity, a person whose "dreams come true"',[10] and yet the reader does not see him realize them. He simply takes his leave of his best friend, Darwin, and vanishes.

Nabokov grants his hero one of his most important facets – acute and rapturous observation. It is this that qualifies him as a visionary and although he is not an artist, he lives equally in his imagination, an imagination fed by the fantastic tales told to him as a little boy by his mother. The 'fun of *Glory*', therefore, lies 'elsewhere'. This initially applies directly to Martin's experience, to his sense that there is something else, something elusive beckoning him, teasing him, a 'magical and demanding impulse, the presence of something for which alone it was worth living'.[11] At the same time it refers to a process to which both Martin and the reader are subject – the 'echoing and linking of minor events', the 'back-and-forth switches which produce the illusion of impetus', the 'masquerade' that is, essentially, Martin's life and Nabokov's text.[12]

Martin is driven by a 'magical and demanding impulse' to escape into an 'unknown land', a dream instilled in his earliest consciousness by an English fairy tale about a boy who climbs into the picture above his bed and 'onto the path that disappeared into

the woods'.[13] Martin has a similar painting in his room, as did
Nabokov at Vyra, and it was the exact same story, read to Vladimir
by his mother, which inspired him, also, to imagine 'the motion'
of 'plunging into that enchanted beechwood'.[14] The 'illusion of impetus' generated by Martin's pursuit of this path, and the recurrence
of mysterious, 'emblematic'[15] paths and trails throughout the novel
culminates in the final path he is to follow into Russia that is only
ever alluded to in the text. It is Darwin who picks up an actual
parallel, 'dark path', one which passes between 'tree trunks in
picturesque and mysterious windings' leading to Martin's family
home where he is to break the news of his disappearance. That this
is all somehow part of the prophetic pattern that Martin perceives
to be shaping his life is implied by the image of the muddy 'impressions' of Darwin's shoes that echo a scene imagined by Martin two
years before, in which he pictures the postman's 'blue footprints'
in the snow as he approaches the same gate.[16]

Glory was not well received. Reviewers commented on the
'brilliance' of its 'formal mastery', on its 'wealth of physiological
vitality', but concluded that these superficial qualities concealed
an 'inner irrelevance', a 'void'.[17] Nabokov's omission of the details
of Martin's fate magnifies this sense of emptiness, and yet this is
'precisely the point', for the 'very absence of the expected "main
part of the text" . . . becomes the fulfillment of his story'.[18] The
void is the novel's central theme, the 'elsewhere' that beguiles and
impels Nabokov's hero and transforms his mundane world into
something vital, urgent and unpredictable. At the same time, the
means by which Martin realizes his dream exposes the artifice that
is the novel itself. His unseen crossing of an invisible border between
Europe and the Soviet Union parallels the 'erosion of the border . . .
between the fictional world and the mind of its author',[19] establishing an involute relationship between author and subject that
was to become a critical and highly potent aspect of Nabokov's
future work.

Within weeks of finishing *Glory*, Nabokov turned to a new idea that would revisit the theme of blindness first introduced in *King, Queen, Knave*, as well as the destructive, three-way relationship at the novel's heart, but now depicted in a far more ruthless scenario. Whereas before, blindness as an ironic dynamic radiated from the myopic Franz, in *Laughter in the Dark* it is focused solely, and with catastrophic consequences, on a middle-aged, Berlin-based art dealer. Albinus begins an affair with a cinema usherette, Margot Peters, who in turn resumes a relationship with a former lover, Axel Rex. When Albinus is blinded in a car accident the two decide to torture and rob him. Albinus discovers the betrayal and attempts to shoot Margot, but is overpowered and killed. Both Nabokov's vicious, insolent heroine and her sadistic lover escape unpunished.

Nabokov was criticized for the novel's relentless cruelty, but he responded that he had only 'tried to express a world in terms as candid, as near to my vision of the world, as I could. If I was cruel, I suppose it was because I saw the world as cruel in those days.'[20] The story seems devoid of morality, and yet there exists another, inverse, three-way relationship – that of Albinus's wife, Elisabeth, his daughter, Irma and brother-in-law, Paul – that lies behind the foregrounded drama, which sets it in stark relief. These characters suffer more because they are innocent, and the prime victim of this scenario is Irma, who dies as a direct result of her father's neglect. Albinus's moral, spiritual and physical weakness re-emerges in subsequent characterizations – the compromised Krug in *Bend Sinister*, who by refusing to acknowledge his vulnerability fails to protect his son, *Lolita*'s Humbert, who destroys a child's life because he is unable to control his paedophilic impulses and *Ada*'s Van Veen, whose oblivious emotional and psychological abuse of his half-sister Lucette drives her to suicide.

The novel first appeared in serialized form in 1932 under the title *Kamera obskura*. It was also the first of Nabokov's novels to

Kamera obskura by
V. Sirin´, 1933.

appear in English, with Hutchinson publishing their own translation in 1935. Two years later, the US publisher Bobbs-Merrill agreed a $600 fee for the rights. Nabokov, dissatisfied with the Hutchinson translation, set about producing his own English version, now with an American audience and Hollywood, particularly, in mind. As well as changing his characters' names he gave the novel a new title: *Laughter in the Dark*. Both titles point to cinema as a critical thematic, stylistic and structural device. Nabokov 'wanted to write the entire book as if it were a film' with 'the scenes and dialogue [following] a cinematic pattern'. 'I wasn't thinking of the form of a screenplay,' he explained, 'it's a verbal imitation of what was then termed a "photoplay".'[21] That he was fascinated by this relatively new creative medium is evident in the way in which he continued to incorporate cinematic techniques and perspectives into his fiction. As he was to later concede, the 'basic idea, [of] my constantly introducing cinema themes, and cinema lore, and cinema-metaphors into my literary compositions cannot be contested'.[22] An avid movie-goer, Nabokov delighted in cinema as a source of pure entertainment, but had little patience for 'the grotesqueness of cinematic cliché'. Friends recalled the way he would 'single out intentionally an inept American film' and 'literally shake with laughter, to the point where . . . he would have to leave the hall'.[23] Since his arrival in Berlin, Nabokov had been producing scenarios for the screen, but in January 1932 he was approached directly for the rights to a recent story, 'The Potato Elf'. Sergey Bertenson, a former Moscow Art Theatre director, introduced him to the Russian-born Hollywood producer/director Lewis Milestone who had just won a second Academy Award for his adaptation of Erich Maria Remarque's *All Quiet on the Western Front*. Nabokov 'grew very excited' at Milestone's proposals, telling Bertenson that 'he literally adore[d] the cinema and watch[ed] motion pictures with great keenness'.[24] Although Milestone's interest came to nothing, it nevertheless signalled to Nabokov the real possibility of having his work brought to an international audience via the silver screen. In terms of his art, the camera eye offered the potential for new perspectives and perceptual possibilities – for new ways and means of seeing.[25]

In the meantime, despite mixed reviews, interest in Nabokov's work was growing steadily. He gained another supporter in December 1931, when the Soviet writer Evgeny Zamyatin arrived in Berlin, declaring him 'a dazzling talent, the greatest acquisition of émigré literature'.[26] In April 1932 Nabokov travelled to Prague to visit his family. All the while he was 'storing impressions for the beginning of his next novel'[27] which he began on his return to Berlin the following month. By the end of the summer he was busy finishing the first draft.

Set once again in contemporary Berlin, *Despair* is cast as the memoir of a Russian-German chocolate salesman. Finding himself on the run in the Pyrenees after murdering a tramp, Felix, who he believes is his double, Hermann decides to write his own version of events – a distorted confession of vaunted hubris, paranoia, 'delusion, desperation, false doubles and Dostoevsky'.[28] According to Nabokov, *Despair* contains 'many entertaining conversations', whilst the 'final scene with Felix in the wintry woods is of course great fun'.[29] These obtuse comments mischievously circumvent the novel's gothic darkness, the extent of Hermann's psychotic 'beastliness',[30] and the cold-blooded horror of Felix's murder. Irony, combined with 'shifts (and hence . . . "shiftiness") in time, memory, consciousness and intention', permeates Hermann's narrative, undermining his every statement, his every move. 'Ostensibly, Hermann is "wrong" about just about everything of any conse-quence',[31] and yet the reader is drawn into his world to such an extent that it is only when an alternative narrative voice intervenes that the reader's perspective is reconfigured and the existence of a tangible counter-reality revealed. Nabokov once commented that 'we dream our own selves'.[32] Hermann Karlovich's dream-self is the nightmarish fantasy of a dangerous, narcissistic egomaniac.

Hermann's most obvious antecedent can be found in Pushkin's 1833 story, 'The Queen of Spades'. Pushkin's hero is a German called Hermann and, like Hermann Karlovich, suffers the 'im-possibility' of reconciling two conflicting halves.[33] As Pushkin's narrator states: 'Two *idées fixes* cannot co-exist in the moral world any more than two physical bodies can occupy one and the same space.'[34] *Despair* also explicitly engages, despite Nabokov's derog-atory statements concerning his least favourite author,[35] with three of Dostoevsky's major works – *Crime and Punishment*, *The Double*, and the raving narrative of *Notes from Underground*. Its manic surrealism is distinctly reminiscent of Gogol's St Petersburg tales, particularly 'The Nose' and 'The Overcoat', whilst notions of the 'arbitrariness – and potential fluidity – of personal identity'[36] find their progenitor in 'The Diary of a Madman'. The genre of the diary, memoir or note in Russian literature ranges from Gogol and Dostoevsky to Saltykov and Bely. Hermann self-consciously and deliberately establishes his connection with this tradition through direct allusion to Tolstoy's 'Notes of a Madman' and Turgenev's *The Diary of a Superfluous Man*.[37] His relationship with these texts is one of both attraction and antagonism, of sustained, unresolved ambivalence. He is compelled to define himself in terms of the fictional characters they portray, and yet he rejects them as worthless and inferior, denying the comparison, as he rejects any possible association with his murderous peers.

Hermann's desire for public recognition torments him, but his 'real anguish' derives from his fear of being 'lumped with "ordinary" criminals',[38] of having the masterful artistry of his crime undermined by banal comparison with 'this or that oaf with vampirish tastes', or 'that fellow who burned his car with his victim's body inside'.[39] Hermann is referring here to two real-life precedents. The 'Düsseldorf Vampire' was a serial killer who, in 1929, 'launched a rampage of terror' that ended with his arrest the following year. Meanwhile, Erich Tetzner initiated a cumbersome insurance scam by faking his own death, and it is this that most closely resembles Hermann's scenario.[40] Both cases generated sensational coverage in the German press, and were also reported extensively in the Russian émigré paper, *Rul´*. By having Hermann refer to the accounts that helped shape his novel, Nabokov merges the fictional with the actual.

Whilst the textual overlapping of Nabokov's and Hermann's worlds reinforces the involutionary relationship between author and subject, it also establishes both Nabokov's role in creating Hermann's scenario and his omniscient presence. Nabokov reveals his 'sovereignty' as 'authentic creator' of 'his character's discourse'[41] by encoding his name in the text, a technique that he deployed throughout his fiction. For example, the Russian for lilac, a dominant colour in Hermann's narrative, is *siren´*, which almost exactly replicates Nabokov's pen-name, Sirin. Its recurrence serves as an indication of Nabokov's presence, and in its echo of the 'lilac worlds' of Russian symbolist poetry and art,[42] is strongly suggestive of a transcendental space that lies beyond the confines of mortal (i.e. Hermann's) apprehension. As it is across his fiction, Nabokov's colour symbolism is neither fixed nor reductive. Here, lilac also serves an extended function in terms of the novel's dense patterning of literary allusions.

Despair's allusive range reaches beyond Russia to England and America, to stories by Conan Doyle, Mayne Reid and Oscar Wilde.[43] Resonances with Wilde's *The Picture of Dorian Gray*, for example, extend from Hermann's preoccupation with mirrors, portraits and reflective surfaces to recurring lilac imagery, which explicitly connects Hermann's narrative with Wilde's story and his self-conscious emulation of Wilde and his protagonist, Lord Henry. Once again, Nabokov discreetly asserts his presence by generating irony through Hermann's deliberate echo of Lord Henry's famous contention on art and class: 'to the lower orders, crime [is] what art is to us, simply a method of procuring extraordinary sensations.'[44] Hermann, in his compulsion to self-aggrandize, blithely merges the two – 'let us discuss crime' he says, 'crime as an art'.[45] What he fails to acknowledge, however, is Lord Henry's preamble – 'All crime is vulgar, just as all vulgarity is crime' – which parallels Nabokov's condemnation of crime as 'a sorry farce'.[46] Instantly, Hermann's assumed stature is undermined, his act exposed as cheap and despicable and his pompous posturing vacuous and reprehensible.

Hermann's creative impulse involves a process of 'self-transformation and self-divestment' which is enabled by his self-projection onto his perceived double. By killing Felix, Hermann essentially cancels himself out, he 'eradicates his own status as a literary character' in order to begin 'a new life as a literary creator'.[47] Hermann's aspiration to merge with a twin image echoes Smurov's solipsistic quest in *The Eye*, and recurs repeatedly throughout the narrative, whilst his desire for self-dispersal and, ultimately, self-annihilation is most eloquently expressed by his depiction of leaves falling on water:

> Below, on the still surface of the water, we admired the exact replica . . . of the park's autumn tapestry . . . When a slow leaf fell, there would flutter up to meet it, out of the water's shadowy depths, its unavoidable double. Their meeting was soundless, the leaf came twirling down, and twirling up there would rise towards it, eagerly, its exact, beautiful, lethal reflection.[48]

Hermann's romantic imagination – which 'hanker[s] after reflections, repetitions, masks' – is fascinated by the possibility of a fatal meeting between two identical entities from separate realms, a meeting that will, however, necessitate the destruction of one or other of them. When confronted by Felix, 'his own shadow, falling dead at his feet' in a 'dark', 'vibrating wood', the image he sees is not the expected one of serenity and beauty, but a face that is 'slowly dissolving' like a fading, distorted reflection 'in a stagnant pool'.[49] Hermann's masterpiece is instantly soured whilst his attempt to salvage it in the realm of letters only serves to expose his malignant lunacy.

In October 1932 Nabokov made his first trip to Paris where he had been invited to give readings of his work. There he enjoyed the hospitality of both the Russian and French literary elite. He stayed with his cousin, the composer, Nicolas Nabokov, saw his brother, Sergey, and visited his friend Ivan Lukash. The trip was an enormous success. Nabokov was 'simply amazed' by the 'wonderfully disinterested, tender attitude everyone has shown me'.[50] By the end of November he was back in Berlin, determined that he and Véra should move to Paris as soon as possible. As it was, they weren't to leave until circumstances eventually gave them no choice.

As Nabokov began work on what was to be his ninth novel, *The Gift*, Hindenburg appointed Hitler as Chancellor. Within months the legalized persecution of Jews began, with Jewish businesses boycotted or shut down by Nazi storm troopers. Véra lost her secretarial job but managed to continue working as a stenographer and interpreter. Meanwhile, Nabokov spent much of 1933 researching the two biographical sections of *The Gift*, that of the nineteenth-century radical socialist, Nikolay Chernyshevsky, and an account by the novel's central protagonist, Fyodor Godunov-Cherdyntsev, of his father's scientific expeditions. *Despair* had appeared as excerpts in *Poslednie novosti* and the following year was serialized, fully, in *Sovremennye zapiski*. In April 1933 Nabokov wrote to fellow émigré and friend Gleb Struve, now a professor of Russian at London University, asking if he could help him find an English publisher. Nabokov was not only keen to be published in Britain, but also to start writing in English. He approached *Poslednie novosti* to see if they would print an English story, but they refused. By the following year, however, Hutchinson had agreed to publish both *Laughter in the Dark* and *Despair*. An American agent was secured and Nabokov's work finally began to make an impact across the Atlantic. 1934 was also a momentous year for another, quite distinct but no less important reason – the birth of Vladimir and Véra's first and only child, Dmitri.

Nabokov was to devote the final chapter of his autobiography to his son's precious early years, prompting him to explain the scope of his feeling:

> Whenever I start thinking of my love for a person, I am in the habit of immediately drawing radii from my love – from my heart, from the tender nucleus of a personal matter – to monstrously remote points of the universe.[51]

Nabokov with his baby son, Dmitri, 1934/5.

Whilst the chapter is full of Dmitri, Véra only materializes as an anonymous 'you'. Rather than a gesture of exclusion, it signals Nabokov's abiding impulse to protect the privacy of his personal relations. Although the characters of his past life are described in vibrant detail, he makes pains to guard his protagonists' true identities. Dmitri's autonomy is ensured by the fact that his childhood is also part of a lost past, and thus his adult persona is in no way compromised by his father's adoring depictions. *Speak, Memory* ends in 1940 as the Nabokovs prepare to sail to America. Whereas Vladimir's former loves and his son's European childhood are left behind, relegated, as it were, to history, Véra remains as a constant, an integral and inextricable part of Nabokov's present life and thus closed to public scrutiny. In this last chapter of his autobiography, Nabokov offers a rare insight into the most intensely personal aspect of his being:

When that slow-motion, silent explosion of love takes place in me, unfolding its melting fringes and overwhelming me with the sense of something much vaster, much more enduring and powerful than the accumulation of matter or energy in any imaginable cosmos, then my mind cannot but pinch itself to see if it is really awake. I have to make a rapid inventory of the universe . . . I have to have all space and all time participate in my emotion, in my mortal love, so that the edge of its mortality is taken off, thus helping me to fight the utter degradation, ridicule, and horror of having developed an infinity of sensation and thought within a finite existence.[52]

Much as his love is expressed in an 'infinity of sensation', so the major themes of his work also reflect this impulse for expansion, for a reaching beyond the confines of mortality to attain a state of universal permanence in a 'free world of timelessness'.[53]

In the eight years since the publication of 'Terror', Nabokov had written a further 21 short stories. Publishing stories was a useful means of boosting his income, but they were also crucial as a medium in which Nabokov could experiment and work through the themes and ideas that informed his longer fiction. The last two stories of the 1930s, 'Ultima Thule' and 'Solus Rex', were to be the preliminary chapters of a final, but eventually abandoned Russian novel, 'garbled echoes'[54] of which resonate in three subsequent English works, *Bend Sinister*, *Pnin* and *Pale Fire*. 'The Circle' (1934) serves as an important precursor to *The Gift*, offering a glimpse into the world of the novel's hero from a 'totally unexpected angle, through the unsympathetic gaze' of a character who makes no appearance in the novel itself.[55] 'Terra Incognita' (1931) also prefigures *The Gift*, as it recounts (in a pre-death hallucination), the disastrous expedition of a team of naturalists to an exotic, remote and hostile territory. The narrator's fever converts itself into the stifling heat of the rainforest, and the scene he envisages is so vivid that the real scenario – of a fatally ill man lying, delirious, in his death-bed – only barely impinges on the drama that is taking place under 'that wonderful, frightening, tropical sky'.[56] This sense of actuality subsumed by a surreal, but highly evocative and convincingly palpable world was to feature in Nabokov's next major novel, *Invitation to a Beheading*.

Meanwhile, themes of angels and ghosts and the possible existence of a spiritual afterlife re-emerge. In 'A Busy Man' (1931), the 'gentle-tempered and death-fearing' Grafitski[57] is granted a continuation of life beyond his 33 years by an angel masquerading as his neighbour. Graf gains only an inkling of Engel's possible interference in a dream and yet Nabokov places a key motif in the text – a rainbow – which signals emphatically to the reader the presence of ethereal forces:

> when Graf woke up the lovely June sun was lighting rainbows in the landlady's liqueur glasses, and everything was somehow soft and luminous and enigmatic – as if there was something he had not understood.[58]

In 'Perfection' (1932), the drowning Ivanov's faulty eyesight is miraculously transformed into the vision of a soaring, discarnate being, and through a sudden, subtle shift in perspective, Nabokov rescues his protagonist from the terror and pain of death. Just as his heart gives out and he begins to drown, Ivanov is transported to the shore, where 'sand, sea, and air were of an odd, faded, opaque tint, and everything was perfectly still'. That Ivanov is already dead is signalled to the reader by his sudden, overwhelming sense of sadness – 'and he felt what he knew from *earthly* life – the poignant heat of tears'[59] – and yet Ivanov believes himself to still be alive. This same misapprehension occurs in a much earlier story, 'Details of a Sunset' from 1924, in which Mark Standfuss is hit by a tram:

Several odd things occurred simultaneously: from the front of the car, as it swayed away from Mark, the conductor emitted a furious shout; the shiny asphalt swept upward [and] a roaring mass hit Mark from behind. He felt as if a thick thunderbolt had gone through him from head to toe, and then nothing. He was standing alone on the glossy asphalt. He looked around. He saw, at a distance, his own figure . . . walking diagonally across the street as if nothing had happened. Marveling, he caught up with himself in one easy sweep, and now it was he nearing the sidewalk, his entire frame filled with a gradually diminishing vibration.[60]

As in 'Terra Incognita', the real world impinges on the imagined world of a dying man. Like Ivanov, Mark suddenly gains a privileged visual perspective, becoming conscious for the first time of the sunset's 'glorious light' playing on the rooftops. His enchanted state is, however, sporadically disrupted by 'bolts' of 'atrocious' pain, reminiscent of the 'spark of Bengal light, crackling and quivering' along a tram cable that opens the story. This electrical spark becomes emblematic of Mark's spirit which is now speeding 'into the distance like a blue star'.[61] Mark's accident is dramatized as a corporeal shift but, as in 'Perfection', it is the synchronous perceptual shift that renders him oblivious to the full horror of his imminent demise. At the same time, the sense of release and the prospect of transference into another dimension offered by this altered perspective is a key element in the elaboration of Nabokov's metaphysics, most explicitly demonstrated by Cincinnatus's fantastic escape at the end of *Invitation to a Beheading*.

In June 1934, Nabokov set aside his work on *The Gift* to start another new novel, finishing a first draft in 'one fortnight of wonderful excitement and sustained inspiration'.[62] *Invitation to a Beheading*, Nabokov was later to comment, 'deals with the incarceration of a rebel in a picture-postcard fortress by the buffoons and bullies of a Communazist state'.[63] Although he was to deny the significance of the political backdrop against which it is set, the novel presents Nabokov's most lurid vision of the 'dull beastly farce' of institutionalized repression.[64] It is a theme that recurs in two other stories of the 1930s – 'Cloud, Castle, Lake' (1937) and 'Tyrants Destroyed' (1938) – as well as *Bend Sinister*, written in America during the last years of the Second World War. Indeed, Nabokov described both *Invitation to a Beheading* and *Bend Sinister* as 'the two bookends of grotesque design between which my other volumes tightly huddle'.[65] In the wider context of contemporary fiction, *Invitation* belongs to the series of dystopian fables initiated by H. G. Wells's *The Sleeper Awakes* (1910) – Zamyatin's *We* (1921), Aldous Huxley's *Brave New World* (1932) and George Orwell's *1984* (1949). Nevertheless, Nabokov made pains to enforce the distinction of his work from any specific genre, resisting all comparison with 'political novels and the literature of social intent'. 'Nothing bores me more', he would retort.[66]

On one level, the purpose of *Invitation* is to expose evil as farce, to render 'iniquity absurd',[67] to prove that 'tyrants and torturers will never manage to hide their comic stumbles behind their cosmic acrobatics', but Nabokov also described it as his 'dreamiest and most poetical novel'.[68] Cincinnatus C., 'a lone, dark obstacle' in a world of 'transparent souls', has been condemned to death for the crime of 'gnostical turpitude'[69] and is incarcerated in a vast prison awaiting execution. The sole inmate, he is presided over by his jailer, the prison director, his lawyer, the director's daughter, and a spider. He is visited by his wife, her lover, her family, her two illegitimate children and his estranged mother. On day five he is introduced to Monsieur Pierre, who initially claims to be a fellow prisoner but turns out to be his executioner. Sentimental, crude, self-righteous, conceited, obsessed with petty trivia and phoney superstitions, Monsieur Pierre epitomizes the very worst aspects of *poshlost*, and Cincinnatus has no defence against the tyranny of his irrational, egocentric, highly manipulative, malicious games. Finally, on day nineteen, Cincinnatus is paraded through town to the scaffold, cheered by excited crowds. As the axe is about to fall, Cincinnatus suddenly splits in two; one version of him remains prone on the block whilst the other walks away as the scene around him collapses like a stage set.

Cincinnatus's dilemma enacts the novel's epigraph: 'Comme un fou se croit Dieu, / nous nous croyons mortels.'[70] Whilst he believes himself to be mortal, and suffers an abject, 'choking, wrenching, implacable' fear of an imminent, violent death, he also knows that he has been 'duped'. The 'gnostical turpitude' that has condemned him grants him an awareness of the fragility of his material world and a spiritual certainty that his present predicament is nothing more than 'pathetic' theatre. He knows that there is something else, 'something genuinely alive, important and vast', that lies behind this ludicrous facade, something that he can sense through its discernable cracks, and yet it eludes him. At the same time, the corporeal split that occurs at the end of the novel is dramatized, in fleeting episodes throughout the narrative, as a pre-existing state. Cincinnatus has a 'precious quality', a 'fleshy incompleteness', a duality of form such that 'the greater part of him was in a quite different place, while only an insignificant portion of it was wandering, perplexed, here':[71]

It seemed as though at any moment . . . Cincinnatus would step in such a way as to slip naturally and effortlessly through some chink in the air into its unknown coulisses to disappear there with the same easy smoothness with which the flashing reflection of a rotated mirror moves across every object in the room and suddenly vanishes, as if beyond the air, in some new depth of ether.[72]

The possibility of transition into this other dimension is evoked by the mere sensation of a change in the current of air, a new draught, reminiscent of the 'leakings and drafts' that infiltrated the not particularly 'solid walls' of Nabokov's own consciousness. These revelations are, however, fleeting, glimpsed only momentarily like a flash of light in another's eyes, seen 'just for an instant . . . as if something real, unquestionable . . . had passed through, as if a corner of this horrible life had curled up, and there was a glimpse of the lining'.[73]

In Cincinnatus's patently artificial world, 'authenticity is creativity'.[74] Surrounded by dead-ends and trap-doors, collapsing rooms and vanishing objects, his only reality is self-expression, and so he keeps a diary, with each chapter corresponding to each day of his incarceration. The passage of time is marked by his ever-decreasing pencil, his writing initiating a 'process of gradual divestment' whereby he senses himself 'taking off layer after layer' until he reaches 'a final, indivisible, firm, radiant point' – his true self.[75] Countering Cincinnatus's private spiritual progress are the daily humiliations, disappointments and betrayals he suffers at the hands of his jailers and his family. This cycle is broken on the final day, when a moth (an Emperor) escapes from his cell. As in 'Christmas', this creature is distinctly emblematic of the 'soul's transcendency',[76] a notion made explicit at the end of *Bend Sinister*, when the author (Nabokov) hears a 'sudden twang' at his 'bright window'. The 'big moth', 'clinging with furry feet', its 'marbled wings' 'vibrating', is the 'rosy soul' of Krug's dead wife 'bombinat[ing] in the damp dark'.[77] Cincinnatus's moth, which 'represents grace and beauty and art at their highest',[78] signals the potential to enter a world of 'radiant, tremulous kindness', a world that presents a distinctly antithetical '*there*' to the nightmare of his 'here'.[79]

Throughout his fiction Nabokov emphasized death as a form of 'divestment' or 'communion',[80] a 'transition from circumscribed awareness to omniscience' whereby 'infinite consciousness' and 'perfect knowledge' are attained.[81] Cincinnatus begins this process of divestment long before he knows when he is to die, but it is significant that it coincides with his impulse to write. Nabokov described the creative process, or the 'inspiration of genius', as a fusion of memory, present experience and imagination which 'come together in a sudden flash':

> The entire circle of time is perceived, which is another way of saying that time ceases to exist. It is a combined sensation of having the whole universe entering you and of yourself wholly dissolving in the universe surrounding you. It is the prison wall of the ego suddenly crumbling away with the nonego rushing in from the outside to save the prisoner – who is already dancing in the open.[82]

Cincinnatus is the prisoner dancing in the open. Gone, also, is the anxiety of 'absolute nothingness'. He erases the last word of his diary – 'death' – and in doing so, cancels it out – 'minus by minus equalled plus, everything was restored, everything was fine'. The novel closes with Cincinnatus moving towards the sound of familiar voices, of 'beings akin to him',[83] implying that his struggle to find his 'own autonomous voice' has finally ended.[84]

Initial responses to *Invitation* were confused. Its nightmarish scenario of surreal entrapment uncannily echoes Franz Kafka's *The Trial* (1925), but Nabokov denied any knowledge of the book, insisting that he 'had no German, was completely ignorant of modern German literature, and had not yet read any French or English translations of Kafka's works'.[85] At the same time, the novel's absurd, farcical quality is reminiscent of Alice's confusing, frustrating trials in Lewis Carroll's nonsensical Wonderland. Reviewers were perplexed. 'What is this? Why was this book written?', wrote Natalya Reznikova:

> It's clear that Sirin is seeking new paths. But it is no less clear that he has wandered into a blind alley. . . . An inexorable book, a terrifying and tormented book.[86]

Once again, Nabokov remained undaunted and, over the next six years, completed over a dozen stories (including one in French), his 'greatest' Russian novel – *The Gift* – two plays, *The Event* and *The Waltz Invention*, translations of *Kamera obskura* and *Despair*, a novella, *The Enchanter*, and his first novel in English, *The Real Life of Sebastian Knight*. Despite this sustained output, his income remained meagre. The Hutchinson publishing deal, which had initially seemed so promising, was a disappointment. Nabokov's advance for *Despair* and *Laughter in the Dark* amounted to just £80 and there was hardly any revenue from sales. Nevertheless, whilst British publishers treated him with scepticism, the Americans were far more enthusiastic. In late summer 1935, Nabokov was featured in the *New York Times Book Review* – 'our age has been enriched by the appearance of a great writer', it declared.[87] Although immensely encouraging, this made little impact on his situation at home since, in addition to his wife and baby son, he also had his family in Prague to support. Véra attempted to return to work in 1936, when Dmitri

Charlottenburg, 1935.

turned two, but quickly discovered that it was almost impossible to keep a job under the new restrictions. At the same time, as a Russian Jew in Nazi Berlin, her safety could no longer be guaranteed. As it was, Nabokov had already come under attack from the Russian right wing, not merely for being married to a Jew, but also through his association with prominent Jewish émigrés, a reputation compounded by his father's legacy. The increasingly precarious nature of Nabokov's position was made chillingly plain in a vicious article published in the Russian fascist press in 1938:

> There, in the boiling pots, all those 'exercises' by the sirins, the chagals [*sic*], the knuts, the burliuks, and hundreds of others will be cleansed entirely. And all those 'works of genius' will flow where flows all filth, opening passage to fresh, national art.[88]

Shortly after Véra lost what was to be her last job, the head of Hitler's department for émigré affairs appointed Sergey Taboritsky, the man convicted of V. D. Nabokov's murder, as his undersecretary. Taboritsky's new assignment was to 'feret out Jews' whilst creating 'a corps of Russian fascist translators and intelligence agents' to assist in the interrogation of political prisoners.[89] By the autumn of 1936, the department was preparing to introduce the enforced registration of all Russian émigrés. It was now imperative that the Nabokovs get out of Germany. Vladimir began writing letters to friends and colleagues in England and America, begging for work, but to no avail. In the meantime, a reading tour to Belgium and France had been arranged and Nabokov had no choice but to go, setting off for Brussels in January 1937. The tour took him to Paris and then to London, where he hoped, in vain, 'to gain access to the English publishing and film worlds'.[90] In February he returned to Paris, and in May travelled direct to Prague, to visit his family, where Véra and

Nabokov's favourite picture of himself, 1936.

Dmitri were also waiting for him. By July, the Nabokovs were in the South of France, where they stayed for just over a year, finally settling in Paris in October 1938. Despite the constant stream of published and translated works, the serialization of *The Gift* in *Sovremennye zapiski* (minus the censored chapter on Chernyshevsky), and the surprising success of his new commission, *The Event*, for the Russian Theatre in Paris, the Nabokovs lived in 'ghastly destitution'.[91] The American publication of *Laughter in the Dark* in April 1938 had brought in a fraction of the remainder of the original advance after fees and taxes. 'My situation is so desperate,' Nabokov wrote, 'It's a mystery how I exist at all.'[92]

The material strain the Nabokovs were suffering during this time pales, however, in the light of the single, cataclysmic event that was to subsume their personal lives during 1937. Whilst on his reading tour to Belgium and France, Nabokov fell in love with a 'vivacious', 31-year-old divorcée. They had first met when Nabokov was in Paris the year before, and she was there again when he returned the following January. By February they were lovers. Irina Guadanini was a 'highly emotional blond'[93] with a 'fine memory for verse', which Nabokov found very seductive.[94] Not only this, but her family had moved in the same St Petersburg circles as Nabokov's. Her stepfather's brother was a leading CD who had been arrested and executed without trial in January 1918. The incident 'had sent a chill throughout liberal Russia',[95] causing such outrage that Nabokov marked its first anniversary with a poem. The affair was serious and very passionate. Nabokov was wracked with guilt, so much so that he developed psoriasis, whose 'indescribable torments' drove him to the 'border of suicide'.[96] He told Irina that he loved her '"more than anything on earth"', and yet he could not deny that his fourteen-year marriage had been 'utterly "cloudless"'.[97] The lovers wrote to each other obsessively. In Prague Nabokov set up a secret post office address in his grand-mother's name exclusively for their correspondence. Meanwhile, Véra received an anonymous letter exposing the affair. Nabokov denied it but confessed, two months later, in Cannes. Véra stood firm. Her pride would not allow her to countenance the possibility of being replaced, nor would she contemplate relinquishing her marriage at the first sign of trouble. At the same time, she was utterly devoted to Nabokov, and even blamed herself for her hus-band's infidelity. Although Nabokov was desperate to be with Irina, he couldn't bring himself to leave his wife and son. When in August Véra discovered that the two were still corresponding she was en-raged. Nabokov wrote to Irina, describing 'such storms that he thought he would end in a madhouse'.[98] Véra threatened to leave him, and to take Dmitri with her. Confronted with the prospect of losing the two people most precious to him, Nabokov surren-dered. He wrote to Irina telling her they were finished, but this only prompted her to come straight to Cannes to confront him. She sat in vigil at a café near the beach waiting for Nabokov to come down with his son. Later that day they met in a public garden, where Nabokov told her that he couldn't leave his family, that he couldn't make a commitment to her. The next day Irina left for Italy, devastated. The following year she attended another of Nabokov's readings, but they were never to meet again.

By January 1938, within four months of ending his affair, Nabokov had completed his last Russian novel, *The Gift*. Set in Berlin in the mid-1920s, it spans three years in the life of a young émigré writer, Fyodor Godunov-Cherdynstev. *The Gift* is both a *Künstlerroman* and a 'city novel, in the European modernist tradition of Andrei Bely's *Petersburg*, Joyce's *Ulysses*, and Döblin's *Alexanderplatz'*.[99] A story about exile, loss and death, it is, ultimately, 'a declaration of love',[100] a love that encompasses a lost country and its great literary tradition, family, friends and lovers, and the processes of art itself – sensation, inspiration, imagination, self-expression.

Fyodor is one of Nabokov's 'good visionaries'. Like Mark Standfuss, he is constantly distracted by the unusual aspect of his everyday world, but as an artist, a fleeting glimpse or a chance vision of an incidental detail, suddenly 'made strange' by the angle of observation, has the power instantaneously to inspire his poetic imagination, or else transport him back into a rapturous scene from his past life. Like Martin Edelweiss, Fyodor is perpetually teased by the sensation of an elusive, intangible 'something', a barely perceptible elsewhere 'concealed behind all this', which he cannot fully access. Fyodor carries his creative gift like 'an illegal treasure', a secret 'burden',[101] whilst perceiving the world around him, equally, as a gift, a privilege, an abundance of rare yet mundane details he is compelled to record and convey by transforming them into future works. In many ways, *The Gift* itself represents, or at least suggests, the first of these.

The Gift is structured across five chapters. In chapter One, Fyodor anxiously awaits the reception of his first volume of poems.

Nabokov and Dmitri in Menton, 1937.

Meanwhile, his friends the Chernyshevskis are trying to cope with the death of their student son, Yasha, in a botched suicide pact. Alexander Chernyshevski senses the persistent presence of his son's ghost, to a point where it begins to permeate his consciousness. His obsession eventually drives him insane, and he is committed for several months to an asylum where, as 'Chairman of the Society for Struggle With the Other World', he spends his time combating the infiltration of multifarious spirits. He also happens to be distantly related to the nineteenth-century radical author and founder of Russian populism, Nikolay Chernyshevsky, whose seminal novel, *What Is To Be Done?*, written in prison in 1862, became, along with Karl Marx's *Capital*, one of the key inspirational works of the Russian revolutionary movement. Fyodor's irreverent and highly parodic biography of this hero of Soviet ideology comprises chapter Four. Meanwhile, in chapter Two, Fyodor attempts to tackle his own father's biography, but abandons it as an impossible task. Chapter Three opens as Fyodor moves to new lodgings where he will meet his lover and muse, Zina Mertz. The move – 'from Pushkin Avenue to Gogol Street' – is also significant in terms of Fyodor's artistic development, designating his transition from poetry to prose and signalling a shift from the covert embedding of Pushkin in the first part of the novel to the explicit stylistic tribute to Gogol that dominates chapter Three. Chapter Five, whilst reinforcing Fyodor's progress as an artist and his commitment to Zina, 'combines all the preceding themes and adumbrates the book Fyodor dreams of writing some day', the 'remarkable' future novel that is, perhaps, *The Gift*.[102]

The narrative course of Fyodor's life is 'presented in a fragmentary fashion: periods are elided; nested texts blend with the master text; and dream is at times allowed to eclipse reality'.[103] This is compounded by *The Gift*'s five-chapter structure, which generates a prevailing sense of incompleteness. In turn, the various partial and abandoned projects that Fyodor undertakes suggests that

the finished work which seems to be *The Gift* is, in fact, yet
to be written. Recurring patterns of fives further magnify this
sense of something that is not quite attainable. Each time they
occur, the fifth aspect or object remains elusive,[104] and yet in the
novel's final chapter, they come close to a resolution. Whilst walking in Berlin's Grunewald, Fyodor notices a group of five nuns
crossing the park. The vision has a 'staged' quality, but to Fyodor,
it is superlative:

> how much skill there was in everything, what an infinity of grace
> and art, what a director lurked behind the pines, how well every-
> thing was calculated.[105]

In an instant, reality becomes art, and the 'reverse side' of the
material world's 'magnificent fabric' seems to rotate, exposing
the images on its 'front' that would otherwise remain 'invisible'.
The revelation afforded by the motif here suggests that Fyodor,
like Cincinnatus, has found the 'something' that has up till now
eluded him. Nevertheless, this sense of closure is ultimately defied
by the novel's inconclusive ending, in which the two 'young lovers'
are dismissed to an uncertain fate.[106]

Far from being a negative force, this ambiguity generates a
positive energy, for the shape of *The Gift* resembles an infinitely
turning, open spiral which, in Nabokov's philosophy, generates
a perpetually forward-moving, liberating dynamic:

> The spiral is a spiritualized circle. In the spiral form, the circle,
> uncoiled, unwound, has ceased to be vicious; it has been set free.
> . . . Twirl follows twirl, and every synthesis is the thesis of the
> next series.[107]

The 'magnificent fabric' that separates the material and metaphysical in Fyodor's world echoes the image of the 'varicoloured

screens' that Kern uses to shield himself from 'cosmic drafts'. Fyodor is granted fleeting glimpses of the 'unusual lining' of this 'magnificent fabric', which occasionally 'turns back' a 'corner' in a moment of magical revelation. Fyodor also senses Kern's 'cosmic drafts', but they do not threaten yawning abysses of infinite nothingness, or even the all-consuming intrusiveness of Alexander Chernyshevski's spirit world. Rather, as in 'Natasha' or *Invitation to a Beheading*, the 'other world' exists as a benign, supportive, inspirational presence that 'surrounds us always', a world that seeps into 'our earthly house' like 'air com[ing] in through the cracks'. Whereas Kern fears it, Fyodor embraces the 'strangeness of life',[108] his art enabling him, like Cincinnatus, to move in and out of different dimensions – of the living and the dead, memory and the imagination, past, present and future.

The Gift is woven together with threads of distinctive motifs. As in *Glory*, where footprints and footsteps take on a fatidic significance, here they are combined with water and rainbows to suggest passage into an alternative, ethereal realm, even a life after death, which culminate in Fyodor's dream of his father's return.[109] Rainbows also signal a moment of transcendence or inspiration, combining with shifts in light and darkness in the pivotal scene between Fyodor and Zina in the hallway of their apartment:

> Through the glass the ashen light from the street fell on both of them and the shadow of the iron design on the door undulated over her and continued obliquely over him, like a shoulder-belt, while a prismatic rainbow lay on the wall.[110]

Associated with Nabokov's description in *Speak, Memory* of the storm at the pavilion at Vyra, this scene takes on a particular resonance, but also because Zina, joined to Fyodor by the belt of light, experiences the dissolution that Fyodor so covets. Like Smurov,

Fyodor aspires to a state of disintegration, whereby his soul is 'liberated from the eyesockets of the flesh', and he is transformed 'into one complete and free eye, which can simultaneously see in all directions'. Fyodor almost achieves this 'cosmic synchronisation' under the heat of the Grunewald sun. He senses his body becoming 'moltenly transparent' and experiences a bifurcation, a dissociation, such that his 'personal I' dissolves and is 'assimilated to the shimmer of the summer forest'. Standing with Fyodor in the darkened hallway, Zina too is divested of her corporeality, becoming a ghost in a 'world of shadows'. An unwitting participant in Fyodor's revelation of the 'strangeness of life', Zina is, from this point on, inextricably linked with his creative identity.[111]

Another dominant motif is that of Nabokov's favourite game, chess, which 'plays a dual role', inspiring Fyodor's decision to write the Chernyshevsky biography and providing 'a schematic model' for the novel's plot.[112] The course of Fyodor's relationship with Zina and his development as an artist takes on, retrospectively, the shape of a sequence of moves on a chess board, whilst the calculation of these moves also serves to define Fyodor's creative technique: 'the fine fabric of deceit, the abundance of insidious tries', the 'false trails carefully prepared for the reader'.[113] Chess, therefore, becomes a metaphor for the very process of novelizing:

> Everything had acquired sense and at the same time everything was concealed. Every creator is a plotter; and all the pieces impersonating his ideas on the board were here as conspirators and sorcerers. Only in the final instant was their secret spectacularly exposed.[114]

What is, then, *The Gift*'s spectacular secret? As it turns back in upon itself, like an ever-revolving spiral or Möbius strip,[115] the reader is left to wonder whether this is, after all, Fyodor's prospective novel, or an altogether different work by an anonymous author. The narrative's constantly shifting authorial voices camouflage the presence of another, distinct yet evanescent perspective, the 'shadows of [whose] world extend beyond the skyline of the page'.[116] Manifested – in anticipation of the 'you' of *Speak, Memory* or *Look at the Harlequins!* – as discreet asides to an unidentified 'other' throughout the narrative, it emerges, emphatically and triumphantly, in the novel's closing *Onegin*-styled epigraph.

In many ways, Fyodor's proposal to 'shuffle, twist, mix, rechew and rebelch'[117] every aspect of his autobiography in a future novel mirrors the same processes that Nabokov underwent in producing his fiction. As he revisits and redeploys the themes and imagery of his earlier work, as characters as diverse as Cincinnatus C. and Smurov, Mark Standfuss, Martin Edelweiss, Kern and Ivanov can be identified in aspects of Fyodor's personality, so elements of Nabokov's own experience can be mapped throughout his fiction like 'a certain intricate watermark whose unique design becomes visible when the lamp of art is made to shine through life's foolscap'.[118]

The Gift may have been Nabokov's last novel written in Russian, but it marked a major logistical development in terms of the way he worked. Written using an entirely new technique, it introduced a method of composition he was to carry through to his very last, unfinished novel: 'that of writing with an eraser-capped pencil on index cards'. Since he would have an 'entire book' already held in a 'now transparent, now dimming dimension' of his mind, index cards gave him the freedom to write out of sequence and to build a novel in disparate stages. It also allowed for an element of spontaneity:

> The greatest happiness I experience in composing is when I feel I cannot understand, or rather catch myself not understanding . . . how or why that image or structural move or exact formulation of phrase has just come to me.

Nabokov claimed that this method helped him organize *The Gift*'s diverse range of sources, but it also enabled him to produce a work of unprecedented complexity. In both style and construction, it anticipates his late American fiction. At the very least, it demands a level of engagement whereby the reader can only begin to 'elucidate' what Nabokov once modestly described as 'the wild workings of my not very efficient mind'.[119]

4

Looking to Other Shores, 1938–40

I take a piece of life, coarse and poor, and create from it a delightful legend – because I am a poet. . . . I, a poet, will erect the legend I have created about the enchanting and the beautiful.[1]

Nabokov disliked Paris, calling it the 'gray, gloomy city on the Seine'. For the first six months he lived in a studio flat just off the Étoile with Véra and a boisterous four-year-old Dmitri. Although it was spacious, with one 'huge handsome'[2] main room, a kitchen and a bathroom, the family had to live and sleep in one space. At night, so as not to disturb their little boy, the Nabokovs entertained guests in the kitchen. Vladimir worked in the bathroom, writing on a suitcase propped on the bidet. From summer to autumn 1938 he had been working on a new play, *The Waltz Invention*, for the Russian Theatre in Paris. Revisiting the themes of *Invitation to a Beheading*, 'Cloud, Castle, Lake' and 'Tyrants Destroyed', and in the wake of Hitler's coercive expansion into Austria, Czechoslovakia and Lithuania, the play depicts a nightmarish scenario of power abused. Its planned premiere in December 1938 never took place, abandoned when the director walked out following a row with the theatre management. It was finally staged 30 years later by the Oxford University Russian Club.

In Paris Nabokov was one of the most exciting figures on the Russian émigré scene. In this 'first flush of [his] so-called fame', he saw himself as a modest figure commanding a loyal, if somewhat marginalized, following:

> Just before World War II around, say, 1938, in Paris where my last novel written in Russian started to run in an émigré magazine I used to visualize my audience with tender irony, as a small group of my émigré fans, each with one of my books held in his hands like a hymnal, all this in the rather subdued light of a back room in a café.[3]

France was, however, a dead end, since Nabokov had been refused a work permit. This, set against the looming threat of Nazi Germany, left him with no alternative but to look for a future beyond Europe. In December 1938 he decided to enter a British literary competition, and at the end of January 1939 submitted his first novel in English, *The Real Life of Sebastian Knight*.

Following the death of his half-brother, the author Sebastian Knight, of a congenital heart condition at 36, V. sets out to write his biography. In part an attempt to rectify the scurrilous and misleading account of Sebastian's life and work by his former secretary, Mr Goodman, V.'s project has a far more personal aspect. Through his investigation into Sebastian's private world, V. hopes to achieve a level of understanding and intimacy that had been perpetually denied him by his 'silent and distant' brother. Nevertheless, V.'s claim to have 'put into this book as little of my own self as possible' is deeply ironic, for *The Real Life of Sebastian Knight* is essentially V.'s account of his pursuit of his brother's ghost. The novel enacts the difficulty of writing a true biography, for 'what you are told is really threefold: shaped by the teller, reshaped by the listener, concealed from both by the dead man of the tale'.[4]

In the process of writing his brother's life, in finding and following the 'undulations' of Sebastian's soul, V. ultimately relinquishes his own identity. By the end of his narrative, the 'mask' of Sebastian 'clings' to his face – 'the likeness will not be washed off' – and the twin images of Sebastian and V. merge – 'I am Sebastian, or Sebastian is I' – making it impossible to distinguish between them. V.'s concluding statement, that 'perhaps we both are someone whom neither of us knows',[5] leaves the reader with the disturbing contention that identities have not merely been lost but altered, irrevocably, or even that this is a scenario in which another distinct but anonymous figure has assumed the brothers' combined identities, a figure who perhaps was also responsible for creating them in the first place and who is, therefore, the ultimate author of V.'s narrative, Vladimir Nabokov.

The Real Life of Sebastian Knight stands out as one of Nabokov's most sophisticated enquiries into authorship and identity. In a talk he gave in Paris in 1937, Nabokov discussed the 'unbridgeable abyss between what is likely (*le vraisemblable*) in fiction, and what is true (*le vrai*) in real life':[6]

> Is it possible to imagine the full reality of another's life, to relive it in one's mind and set it down intact on paper? I doubt it: one even finds oneself seduced by the idea that thought itself, as it shines its beam on the story of a man's life, cannot avoid deforming it. Thus, what our mind perceives turns out to be plausible, but not true.[7]

In its treatment of preoccupying themes of mortality, the supernatural and the otherworld, the novel executes an extraordinary feat of patterning, layering and mirroring whilst engaging directly with a range of literary genres and several major works from the Modernist canon.[8] At the same time, it demonstrates the 'system' which Nabokov outlined to his editor at the *New Yorker* in 1951, of constructing his fiction on multiple narrative planes, whereby a 'second (main) story is woven into, or placed behind, the superficial semitransparent one'.[9] Here, V.'s foregrounded narrative serves as the frame for the novel's second, parallel story which elaborates the extent to which Sebastian's spirit guides his brother in his quest to discover the 'absolute solution'.[10]

Sebastian's presence in V.'s narrative is universal, manifested in the discreet repetition of covert images, themes and motifs – the number 36, the figure of Narcissus, velvet, violet and violets, water (puddles, rivers, rain), snowflakes,[11] mist, fog, rainbows, spiders, chess pieces and chequer boards, trains, even a black bulldog.[12] The colour violet, in particular, is central to notions of transition and transcendence which refer both to V.'s relationship with Sebastian and the stage in Nabokov's art that the novel itself represents. Nabokov's switch from Russian to English can be considered, in respect of his colour-inspired imagination, as emblematized by the place of violet at the end and beginning, respectively, of both the primary and secondary rainbows.[13] In terms of his synaesthetic alphabet, V.'s and Sebastian's initials comprise the two colours – red and blue – that produce violet. Their merging, at the end of the novel, eloquently dramatizes a return to the narrative's predominant cast, at the same time reflecting the single identity of its author, 'V' (Vladimir) and 'S' (Sirin).[14] Violet also complements blue which, in Nabokov's 'chromatic order', is the 'colour of immortality'.[15] With this in mind, episodes in which the colour figures predominantly take on a special significance, in particular V.'s final train journey from Marseille to Paris, during which his carriage is lit by a 'violet-blue night-lamp', and the 'glow' of a 'blue-shaded lamp' that lights the hallway outside the already dead Sebastian's hospital room.[16]

The fundamental ambiguities that lie at the heart of the novel – the questions of Sebastian's true merit as a person and an artist and the nature of V.'s identity – are never resolved. Reports of Sebastian build a picture of an essentially unspectacular character – introspective, solitary, selfish, cold – of dubious talent, described as 'a dull man writing broken English' and, subsequently, 'a broken man writing dull English'.[17] Nabokov's return to the theme of biography that dominated *The Gift* is extended to elements of his own autobiography. Sebastian shares many aspects of Nabokov's life – born in 1899, forced to flee the Russian Revolution, educated at Cambridge, settling in Europe and switching from his native Russian to English, a move that Nabokov made here out of simple expediency, but one that he would soon have no choice but to make permanent. Aspects of Sebastian's relationship with Nina Rechnoy echo the Irina Guadanini affair,[18] and there are also parallels with Nabokov's family, particularly his relationship with his younger brother, Sergey, which was characterized by an awkwardness he was never quite able to reconcile. Nevertheless, the distinctions are sufficient to prevent simplistic, reductive interpretation. In a 1964 interview Nabokov commented that 'people tend to underestimate the power of my imagination and my capacity of evolving serial selves in my writings',[19] but his protagonists also evolve 'serial selves' across his texts. *The Real Life of Sebastian Knight* can be seen as an inverse reflection of *Despair*,[20] whilst its pivotal author/biographer dynamic most overtly prefigures the 1962 novel *Pale Fire*, in which Charles Kinbote assumes intimacy with the poet John Shade, taking on the role of editor after his death, and imposing his autobiography on Shade's life and work in order to assert his own precarious and deeply compromised identity.

In February 1939, the Nabokovs' long-standing friends, Paul and Lucie Léon, invited them to dinner with James Joyce. Nabokov had encountered Joyce in Paris two years before, when he had turned up at a reading Nabokov was giving at the Hungarian consulate. Nabokov had been asked to stand in for a best-selling author, Jolán Földes, who had been taken ill, but at the sight of this stranger, Földes's fans made straight for the exit, leaving behind a motley crowd that included a number of Nabokov's supporters – Denis

Roche, Raisa Tatarinov, Mark Aldanov, Ivan Bunin, Alexander Kerensky, the Léons and James Joyce. Nabokov was delighted:

> A source of unforgettable consolation was the sight of Joyce sitting, arms folded and glasses glinting, in the midst of the Hungarian football team.[21]

Paul Léon had been working closely with Joyce since 1930, and was responsible for his financial and legal affairs, but also advised on translations and new projects. Léon had always been anxious for Nabokov to meet Joyce, and was expecting an occasion of daz-zling intellectual fireworks, but neither man delivered. Nabokov remembered it simply as a 'long friendly evening of talk', admitting that he was 'always a disappointing guest, neither inclined nor able to shine socially'. The only detail of the conversation that Véra could recall was that Joyce was particularly interested in finding out the 'exact ingredients of Russian *myod*', or mead, which nobody could tell him.[22]

Following another unsuccessful job-hunting trip to England in April, Vladimir, Véra and Dmitri moved to a two-room apartment towards the southernmost corner of the 16th arrondissement. News came shortly after that Nabokov's mother had died, but it was far too dangerous for Vladimir to attend the funeral in what was now Nazi-occupied Czechoslovakia. In the meantime, another invitation came through from England, this time for Nabokov to give a talk at Manchester University, but he returned without any prospect of a future there. Nevertheless, there was enough money for the family to take a holiday, and they spent the sum-mer in the French Alps and on the Riviera, heading back to Paris in September. They arrived to the news that Nabokov had been recommended for a job teaching a course in Russian literature at Stanford University in the summer of 1941. Even though it was only a short-term contract, Nabokov accepted it without hesitation,

The Nabokovs' last Paris apartment was destroyed by a bomb on 3 June 1940 in the only German air raid on the French capital of the Second World War.

since it would guarantee him an American visa and passage out of Europe. With Germany's recent invasion of Poland and Britain's declaration of war, organizing their departure was now ever more urgent, but it also meant that it would be a tricky and expensive process. A year before, Sergey Rachmaninov, on hearing of Nabokov's dire financial circumstances, had sent him 2,500 francs.[23] Now, another émigré friend, a cinema-owner, offered to help with a gift of 1,000 francs a month. For the first time in years, Nabokov advertised his services as an English teacher. Despite the difficulties of his day-to-day existence, the inspiration to write had not left him. In October he began work on a new novella, *The Enchanter*.

'The first little throb of *Lolita* went through me late in 1939 or early in 1940 in Paris',[24] Nabokov recalled. Set in an anonymous French town, *The Enchanter* is the story of a paedophile who pursues a twelve-year-old girl he encounters in a park by ingratiating himself with her terminally ill widowed mother. They marry, and a few months later, the woman dies, leaving Nabokov's hero in charge of her daughter. He offers to take her to the seaside, and on the way they stop for the night at a hotel. Finding himself finally alone with the girl, he begins to explore her sleeping body in a slow and meticulous ritual of highly charged eroticism. Just as he reaches sexual climax the girl wakes up and starts screaming. Exposed, embarrassed, ashamed, the man beats a hasty retreat, running out into the road where he is hit and killed by a passing truck.

Nabokov's theme was not new to Russian literature, or even his own fiction. Two of Dostoevsky's major works – *Crime and Punishment* and 'Stavrogin's Confession' from *The Devils* – include actual or imagined abuse of little girls, whilst *Netochka Nezvanova* features a sexually precocious heroine.[25] *The Petty Demon* (1907), by the Symbolist writer Fyodor Sologub, features a subplot in which an older woman erotically fetishizes an adolescent boy. A 'celebrated' and 'notorious' work, it was one of the books in V. D. Nabokov's library.[26] Having been initially suppressed, 'Stavrogin's Confession' was published in March/April 1922, 'simultaneously with the news of the assassination of Nabokov's father'.[27] Meanwhile, Nabokovian predecessors appear in *The Gift*, when Zina's stepfather proposes the very scenario to Fyodor that Nabokov's enchanter will subsequently enact,[28] and in a 1926 story, 'A Nursery Tale', which features 'a somewhat decrepit but unmistakable Humbert escorting his nymphet'.[29]

Some seventeen years later, when writing his afterword to *Lolita*, Nabokov remembered the novella, thinking that he had destroyed it because he had 'not been pleased with the thing'. When a single copy turned up amongst a batch of papers in 1959, he revised his opinion of what he had initially believed to be merely a 'dead scrap', describing it as 'a beautiful piece of Russian prose, precise and lucid'.[30] Obscured by the shadow of *Lolita*, *The Enchanter* has attracted little critical attention, often dismissed as a crude and pale precursor. Stylistically ferocious and grotesquely visceral, it is a narrative of 'intricate metaphorical coordination',[31] deserving of serious consideration as an important work in its own right.

Central to the story's dramatic exposition is the theme of vision – corrupted, distortive and highly selective. Nabokov's hero purports to have 'the keen eye of an appraiser of facets and reflections' (he is a jeweller),[32] but it is focused solely and intently on the object of his passion. The impact of the spectacle of this child is so overwhelming that it obliterates all consciousness of a world apart from her, and he is consumed by his impulse to possess her, utterly. At the same time, his desire is driven by his intense visual apprehension of her physicality, and its effect upon him is palpably catastrophic:

> The girl's arrival, her breathing, her legs, her hair, everything she did . . . evoked an intolerable sensation of sanguine, dermal, multivascular communion with her, as if the monstrous bisector pumping all the juices from the depths of his being extended into her like a pulsating dotted line, as if this girl were growing out of him, as if, with every carefree movement, she tugged and shook her vital roots implanted in the bowels of his being, so that, when she abruptly changed position or rushed off, he felt a yank, a barbarous pluck, a momentary loss of equilibrium: suddenly you are traveling through the dust on your back, banging the back of your head, on your way to being strung up by your insides.[33]

Compounding this theme of narrowed or selective vision, and magnifying the story's dramatic irony, is the recurrence of a series of objects which signal the presence of a 'second' story, 'placed behind' the foregrounded scenario, that suggests the discreet activity of other narrative and metaphysical forces which, however, remain invisible to Nabokov's protagonist.[34] The most eloquent of these is a gold necklace bequeathed to the little girl by her mother – a 'golden little stream of chain (with a cross, probably, or a charm at its end)'[35] – which Nabokov's hero finally notices in the story's closing scenes, as he painstakingly traces every contour of the sleeping girl's body. The necklace, as one of a collection of other apparently insignificant objects, serves as an implicit warning, or impediment, designed to protect the little girl and thwart Nabokov's hero, but is also eloquently suggestive of how far the 'spirits of the dead . . . softly interpose in the affairs of the quick'.[36]

The parallels with *Lolita* are many – a vulnerable young girl, unloved and resented by a widowed mother, a middle-aged man with an unfulfilled obsession, 'the suspicious chauffeur who vaguely foreshadows Clare Quilty',[37] the cars and car crashes, the abortive fairytale fantasy played out in a seedy hotel facilitated by fortuitous twists of fate. Although in the intervening years, *The Enchanter* was to grow 'in secret the claws and wings of a novel',[38] it remains one of the most 'strikingly original'[39] examples of Nabokov's mature Russian work, powerfully compelling in its technical complexity and sheer narrative force.

With affidavits secured from prominent émigrés in the United States, including Nabokov's former art teacher, Mstislav Dobuzhinsky, and the world-renowned Music Director of the Boston Symphony Orchestra, Serge Koussevitzky, Nabokov and Véra spent the last weeks of 1939 desperately trying to acquire all the necessary exit papers, passports and visas for their departure. Whilst compiling the notes for his Stanford lectures, Nabokov had begun work on a new novel, *Solus Rex*. He completed just two chapters before leaving Europe, which were published separately and in reverse order. The second, 'Solus Rex', appeared in *Sovremennye zapiski* in April 1940, but the first, 'Ultima Thule', waited another two years to be published, in New York's *Novyi zhurnal* (*The New Review*). Nabokov insisted that the projected novel 'promised to differ radically, by the quality of its coloration, by the amplitude of its style, by something indefinable about its powerful underflow, from all my other works in Russian'. It is impossible to tell exactly how these qualities would have been elaborated, particularly since the stories themselves differ so radically, but Nabokov's plan was that the fantastical world of 'Solus Rex' – the imaginative construct of an artist searching for a means to distract himself from the grief of losing his wife – should 'develop its own reality', gradually imposing on the contemporary setting of 'Ultima Thule', such that the two worlds become inextricably intertwined, and their respective protagonists fatefully interconnected. However the novel was intended to evolve, Nabokov chose to leave it behind, relegating it to the 'dust and debris' of his 'old fancies'.[40]

In the meantime, he had been approached by Yakov Frumkin, an old friend of his father's, who was now the director of HIAS, a New York-based Jewish charity. HIAS had chartered a ship to evacuate Jewish refugees from Europe in late May and Frumkin offered Nabokov a cabin for half the fare. Friends and associates helped raise the remaining $560. Days after Hitler's tanks began rolling into France, and less than a month before the fall of Paris, the Nabokovs sailed from St Nazaire on what was to be the *Champlain*'s last voyage – it was sunk on its next crossing by a German mine.

5

Becoming Vladimir Nabokov:
Bend Sinister to *Lolita*

I did know I would eventually land in America.[1]

On 28 May 1940, the *Champlain* sailed into New York harbour.
On disembarking, the Nabokovs couldn't find the key to their trunk,
so they chatted with the customs officers until a locksmith arrived
to break it open. A pair of boxing gloves lay on top of their things
and two of the officers picked them up and began sparring, whilst
a third examined a case of butterflies, suggesting a name for one of
its species. They even offered to fetch them a copy of the *New York
Times*. Nabokov was thrilled by all of this, and on the countless
occasions when he retold the story would exclaim, 'Where would
that happen? Where would that happen?' Then, in the taxicab on
the way to their friend's Madison Avenue apartment, they confused
the fare, thinking it was $90 instead of 90 cents. When Véra
proffered a $100 bill, which was almost all the money they had on
them, the cab driver refused it. 'Lady,' he said, 'if I had that kind of
money, I wouldn't be sitting here driving this cab.'[2] As Nabokov
went into his citizenship test in 1945, his friend, Mikhail Karpovich,
begged him to take the occasion seriously. 'Don't joke, please
don't joke with them', he pleaded, but Nabokov couldn't resist
taking advantage of a couple of trivial misunderstandings, and the
proceedings quickly degenerated, with Nabokov and his examiner
collapsing in fits of giggles. Later he declared that he'd had a
'wonderful' time.[3]

In September, the Nabokovs moved into a small apartment on West 87th Street. A few weeks later, at the prompting of his cousin Nicolas, Nabokov called upon the celebrated author and critic Edmund Wilson. Wilson was at the time acting literary editor of the *New Republic*, and suggested Nabokov review for them. He was instantly impressed, describing Nabokov as 'a brilliant fellow'.[4] This was to be the beginning of an 'exhilarating', 'stimulating' but 'restless' friendship that would last over two decades, eventually ending in bitter acrimony following Wilson's attack of Nabokov's translation of *Eugene Onegin*. During this initial 'radiant era',[5] however, Wilson was key in establishing Nabokov on the American literary scene. Soon he was also writing for the *New York Sun* and the *New York Times*, and between giving Russian-language classes

'*Plebejus (Lysandra) Cormion* Nabokov', discovered by Nabokov in July 1938 in the Alpes Maritimes.

to a handful of Columbia students, spent his spare time at the Museum of Natural History, where he had volunteered his services to help organize their butterfly collection. All the while, he was waiting for confirmation of the Stanford summer job, and when it finally came through in the autumn of 1940, he resumed the work he had begun the winter before, researching and writing almost 100 lectures, producing 'about 2,000 pages' of notes and text,[6] as well as translations of poems by Pushkin, Lermontov and Tyutchev. He also published three entomological articles, two based on his work at the Museum of Natural History, and one on an unidentified butterfly he had captured in the Alpes-Maritimes two summers before.

With money still scarce, Nabokov added his name to the lecture-tour roster at the Institute of International Education, giving his first talk at Wells College near Cornell in February 1941. In March New England's Wellesley College invited him to guest lecture for two weeks. They liked him so much they gave him a bonus and offered him a residency for the coming academic year. Whilst in Massachusetts, and at the instigation of Edmund Wilson, Nabokov met Edward Weeks, editor of the *Atlantic Monthly*. Weeks had just read 'Cloud, Castle, Lake' and was 'enchanted'. He called Nabokov a 'genius', and wanted to publish the story immediately along with anything else he could offer, Nabokov was more than merely an extraordinary writer, as Weeks recalled:

He would come in in a shabby tweed coat, trousers bulging at the knee, but be quite the most distinguished man in the room, with his perfectly beautiful hazel eyes, his fine brown hair, the *élan*, the spark . . . He just had to walk into the room and the girls looked around – the clothes didn't make any difference. He had a way of carrying himself, a *joie* in his eyes, a zest.[7]

In the meantime, 'The Event' had its New York premiere at the Heckscher Theatre on Fifth Avenue, with sets designed by Mikhail Dobuzhinsky. Then in April, Rachmaninov, whom Nabokov had finally met a few months before, asked him if he would translate the Russian text of his 1913 choral work, *The Bells*, the original being a 'reckless' adaptation by Bal'mont of a poem by Edgar Allan Poe.[8] This led to further collaboration on a translation of the libretto for his opera, *The Covetous Knight*. Although Rachmaninov was very enthusiastic about both projects, Nabokov's version of *The Bells* was never performed, and Rachmaninov died before work on the libretto translation could be completed.[9]

In May the Nabokovs set off for California. Stanford was unable to help with the travel costs to Palo Alto, so the journey was made by car. The trip was Vladimir's first chance to collect American butterflies and at every stop he ventured forth with his net. In New Mexico he 'was nearly arrested because [he] painted a farmer's trees with sugar to attract a certain type of moth'.[10] At the Grand Canyon he discovered an undescribed species, which he later named *Neonympha dorothea* after his Russian-language student Dorothy Leuthold, who had driven them from East Coast to West.[11]

Nabokov's Stanford classes were on Modern Russian Literature and The Art of Writing, focusing on drama. His opening lectures at Wellesley were, appropriately, on Russian writers as European writers. Nabokov's lecturing style was stimulating, inspiring and highly entertaining. As one of his students explained, he was

as impossible to reduce to notes as to convert a Rolls-Royce into tin cans with a tack hammer . . . It would have been rather like scribbling . . . when Michelangelo talked about how he had designed and painted the ceiling of the Sistine Chapel.

Nabokov, Véra and Dorothy Leuthold (centre), on their way to Palo Alto, 1941.

Nabokov also gave his students precious insights into his compositional methods, including his tactic of mischievously 'lur[ing] the reader this way and that and then tickl[ing] him behind the ear just to see him whirl around'.[12]

In July 1941, *The Real Life of Sebastian Knight* was bought by James Laughlin at New Directions, who went on to commission a volume of translations of Pushkin, Lermontov and Tyutchev and a book on Gogol.[13] Before returning to Wellesley, the Nabokovs travelled up to San Francisco, where Vladimir went butterfly hunting in Yosemite Park, becoming so distracted that he almost tripped over a sleeping bear. In October he took up a Research Fellowship at Harvard's Museum of Comparative Zoology, specializing in the American *Lycaeides* genus of 'silver-studded' blue butterfly. Two summers later, in Utah, Nabokov caught several unidentified species of moth, one of which was subsequently named *Eupithecia nabokovi*, and the following year identified a subspecies which he named the Karner Blue, which has since been classified as a distinct species.[14] In 1951 he discovered the first known female of *Lycaeides sublivens*, the 'Northern Blue' (subsequently named 'Nabokov's Blue'), above

Nabokov at the Harvard Museum of Comparative Zoology.

Telluride, Colorado, in a

> damp, unfrequented, but very spectacular cul-de-sac (which a
> prodigious rainbow straddled every evening) at the end of two
> converging roads, one from Placerville, the other from Dolores,
> both atrocious.[15]

Nabokov described his time in Harvard's 'laboratorial paradise'[16] as 'the most delightful and thrilling in all my adult life'[17] –
his fellowship was renewed every year until his move to Cornell

The Specialist. "THIS IS VERY INTERESTING, BUT I MUST NOT FORGET THAT I CAME HERE TO COLLECT SPECIMENS OF LEPIDOPTERA."

The *Punch* cartoon from above Nabokov's desk at the Harvard Museum.

in 1948. Until then, he eked out a living from various literary grants and fellowships, and what little extra income he could generate from publishing and lecture tours. His 'Chichikov Travels' in the autumn of 1942 took him across America's southern states, where he met 'charming and brilliant people', 'played tennis, canoed, danced' and collected butterflies.[18] From September 1943 he returned to Wellesley to teach Russian, where he quickly settled into a comfortable routine:

> In the morning I peer at the genitalia of butterflies; in the afternoon, I teach Russian grammar to students; . . . in the evening I get into bed with a mug of hot milk and write.[19]

Nevertheless, by early 1944 Nabokov was considering moving to the West Coast, and wrote to a Hollywood agent asking if he could come out to California to be a screenwriter. Then in June things began to turn. Katherine White of the *New Yorker* offered him an advance of $500 against future contributions in return for the rights for first consideration of any new work. He also sold the film rights to *Laughter in the Dark* for $2,500, and in the autumn began a permanent lectureship at Wellesley.

Once in Ithaca, the Nabokovs moved from one rented house to another, occupying a series of homes belonging to Cornell faculty members absent on sabbatical leave. Their favourite was 880 Highland Road, where they lived for a year, from February 1957. The house had a large picture window overlooking a beech wood. 'At night, uncurtained, the window made all the furniture appear to stand out in that crystal land' – a vision that was to inspire the opening stanza of John Shade's poem, 'Pale Fire'. They had a wide circle of friends, and all accounts tell of Vladimir's kindness, accessibility, sensitivity and generosity of spirit, although he was also 'subtle', 'oblique', 'self-mocking and testing all the time'. Colleagues recalled 'his playfulness, his jokes, his word games and puzzles, his uproarious delight at oddities, his loud hearty laugh, the explosions of hilarity that would fill his eyes with tears', and his boundless curiosity.[20]

Despite his enthusiasm for all things American, Nabokov mourned the loss of his native language. 'My private tragedy,' he confessed, 'is that I had to abandon my natural idiom, my untrammelled, rich, and infinitely docile Russian tongue for a second-rate brand of English.'[21] Nevertheless, Nabokov maintained an 'unbroken tie' with his homeland – '-twined solely of love and despair' – by continuing to write poetry in Russian.[22] In a 1942 poem, 'Slava' ('Fame'), he evocatively reasserts the contention that 'words have no borders', first voiced by a grieving father in his 1923 story, 'Gods':

> . . . I kept changing countries like counterfeit money,
> hurrying on and afraid to look back,
> like a phantom dividing in two, like a candle
> between mirrors sailing into the sun. . . .
>
> But my word, curved to form an aerial viaduct,
> spans the world, and across in a strobe-effect spin
> of spokes I keep endlessly passing incognito
> into the flame-licked night of my native land.[23]

Nabokov refused to perceive his situation negatively. Rather, he regarded his 'condition of permanent exile' as the predicament of 'all writers of genius', one that 'with great Russian writers has always been an almost natural state'.[24] Coming to America was simply yet another 'break in [his] destiny' which, like the loss of his homeland, had served to stimulate and enrich his creative imagination.[25] 'Had there been no revolution in Russia,' he argued, 'I would have devoted myself entirely to lepidopterology and never written any novels at all':[26]

America is my home now. It is my country. The intellectual life suits me better than any other country in the world. I have more friends there, more kindred souls than anywhere.[27]

America, that 'cultured and exceedingly diverse country',[28] gave him the freedom he so valued, along with his 'best readers', 'minds' he said, that were 'closest' to his. 'An American writer raised in Russia', he considered himself as 'American as April in Arizona'.[29]

Another tragedy was to cast a deep shadow over Nabokov's first years in America, however. In the autumn of 1945 he dreamed that his brother Sergey was languishing in a German concentration camp. The following day he heard that Sergey had died of malnutrition at Neuengamme labour camp, just outside Hamburg.[30] In 1943 Sergey had been arrested in Berlin for his homosexuality and incarcerated for five months. On his release he went to Prague, where he was informed on for openly condemning the Nazi regime and arrested under the pretext that he was a British spy. Relations between the brothers had always been distant, and whilst the news of Sergey's death was a terrible blow, Nabokov had to concede, remorsefully, that there had never been 'even any friendship' between them – 'it is with a strange feeling that I realise I could describe my whole youth in detail without recalling him once.'[31]

Since arriving in the States, Nabokov had published several new English poems, the first being 'The Refrigerator Awakes' in the *New Yorker*,[32] but in January 1943 his first American story, 'The Assistant Producer', appeared in the *Atlantic Monthly*, and the following summer the *New Yorker* paid over $800 for 'Double Talk' (subsequently retitled as 'Conversation Piece, 1945'). In December 1947 New Directions published Nabokov's first English collection, *Nine Stories*, which included translations of four of his major Russian stories from the 1930s – 'Spring in Fialta', 'Cloud, Castle, Lake', 'The Aurelian', 'A Forgotten Poet' – a translation of a French story, 'Mademoiselle O', from 1936 (which was to become chapter Five of *Speak, Memory*), and four written since his arrival in America – 'The Assistant Producer', 'That in Aleppo Once . . .', 'Time and Ebb' and 'Double Talk'. Just over a decade later, these stories were to reappear in a new collection, *Nabokov's Dozen*, with the addition of 'First Love' (chapter Seven of *Speak, Memory*), 'Signs and Symbols', 'Scenes from the Life of a Double Monster' and Nabokov's last story, 'Lance'.

In June 1946 Nabokov completed his eleventh novel, *Bend Sinister*. He had been working on it, intermittently, for four years, although 'the greater part of the book was composed in the winter and spring of 1945–1946'. It was, Nabokov said,

> a particularly cloudless and vigorous period of my life. My health was excellent. My daily consumption of cigarettes had reached the four-package mark. I slept at least four or five hours, the rest of the night walking pencil in hand about the dingy little flat in Craigie Circle.[33]

Bend Sinister grimly portrays 'certain subtle achievements of the mind in modern times', set 'against a dull-red background of nightmare oppression and persecution'.[34] Although Nabokov deliberately placed 'bits of Lenin's speeches', a 'chunk of the Soviet constitution, and gobs of Nazi pseudo-efficiency'[35] into his narrative, the novel resists classification as a one-dimensional dystopian polemic. In his introduction to its 1963 edition, Nabokov took pains to make his position clear. 'I am not "sincere,"' he argued, 'I am not "provocative," I am not "satirical." I am not a didacticist nor an allegorizer. . . . My characters are not "types," not carriers of this or that "idea."' Rather, as in *Invitation to a Beheading*, the novel's central preoccupation is the very personal dilemma of its hero, the philosopher, Adam Krug – the 'beating' of his 'loving heart' and the 'torture an intense tenderness is subjected to'.[36] Nabokov has often been criticized for his indifference to contemporary issues, but a letter to his sister, written as he was finishing his new novel, reveals an acute awareness of the recent horrors perpetrated by Nazi Germany:

> much as one might want to hide in one's little ivory tower, there are things that torment me too deeply, e.g., the German vilenesses, the burning of children in ovens, – children as funny and as strongly loved as our children.[37]

For Nabokov, despotism was a timeless force to which the events of history simply presented redefined opportunities. In the case of Russia, he posited, 'any changes that took place between November [1917] and now have been changes in the décor which more or less screens an unchanging black abyss of oppression and terror'.[38] Timelessness, however, was also essential to his creativity – 'what makes a work of fiction safe from larvae and rust', he argued, 'is not its social importance but its art, only its art.'[39]

Adam Krug is a philosopher and faculty member at the university in Padukgrad, named after his country's newly installed dictator. As the story opens, Adam is watching his wife, Olga, die in hospital. He returns home to their eight-year-old son, David, and attempts to carry on with his life. Krug is indifferent to the current political climate and Paduk's efforts to bring society into line with his Ekwilist regime. As one of the country's leading and internationally renowned intellectuals, it becomes imperative that Krug comply with the requirements of the state, but he resists all pressure, impervious to bribes and threats, stubbornly implacable in the face of the coercion and arrest of his colleagues until, finally, Paduk takes his son. At first Krug capitulates but then news reaches him that David has been mistaken for another boy, taken to an asylum and killed during a brutal psychiatric experiment. As a last resort, Paduk offers Krug the chance to save 24 of his friends in return for his cooperation, but it is too late – Krug has already lost his mind.

The true author of Krug's world steps in to save him from the 'senseless agony of his logical fate'[40] by first relieving him of his sanity, and then halting the action just as Krug is about to be shot. Although the immortality Nabokov confers upon his hero may be merely a 'slippery sophism' or a 'play on words', it is highly expressive of his assertion of the potential of death to become, in art, simply 'a question of style'.[41]

As if in honour of the Russian meaning of his hero's name (*krug* means 'circle'), the novel has a circular structure, signalled by the 'glint of a special puddle' which appears in its opening and closing paragraphs:

> an oblong puddle inset in the coarse asphalt; like a fancy footprint filled to the brim with quicksilver; like a spatulate hole through which you can see the nether sky.[42]

Critically, however, this apparent cyclic structure is merely a *trompe l'oeil*. The recurrence of the puddle discloses the presence of a third dimension, a distinct actuality that is Nabokov's world. Nabokov makes his presence felt at discreet points throughout the narrative, emerging fully in the story's closing moments. He saves his hero from a 'better bullet' by simply cancelling the scene, 'like a rapidly withdrawn slide',[43] much in the same way that Cincinnatus's world disintegrates as the executioner's axe falls. Here, however, Nabokov leaves no doubt as to the arbiter of Krug's salvation. With the novel's inherent fictionality exposed, its closed and 'vicious' world is 'set free', it 'uncoils' and 'unwinds' to become an open spiral, in a dramatic enactment of Nabokov's 'spiritualized circle'.[44]

Bend Sinister presents yet another development in the design of Nabokov's fiction, whereby a 'second (main) story is woven into, or placed behind, the superficial semitransparent one', and the puddle theme is crucial in the elaboration of this design. Combining the footprint motif from *Glory* and the notion of puddles serving as 'apertures onto some other heavens' first introduced in the 1923 story, 'Sounds', it establishes the 'rent' in Krug's universe that reveals an alternate 'world of tenderness, brightness and beauty'.[45] Acting alongside this third, authorial dimension is a fourth, 'superhigh level of art', which Nabokov had recently identified in Gogol's work. At this level, he argued, literature 'appeals to the secret depth of the human soul where the shadows of other worlds pass like the shadows of nameless and soundless ships'.[46] Deploying both the metaphysical and the metafictional – narrative 'pulsations', stream-of-consciousness, linguistic play, motifs of rainbows, puddles and moths, and a network of literary allusions ranging from Shakespeare to Joyce – the shadows of this fourth dimension evocatively express the measure of Krug's soul, but also magnify the sense of his world as essentially ephemeral.[47] This is not to undermine his predicament but rather to establish 'a certain very special quality' which is 'in itself a kind of justification and redemption'.[48] Whilst Nabokov takes pity on his tormented hero by obliterating 'his remembered hideous misfortune',[49] he is at the same time saving him from the realization of his own culpability in his son's murder. By retreating to the safety of his ivory tower and refusing to recognize the magnitude of the danger confronting him, Krug forgot that his child would be rendered vulnerable too and failed, tragically, to acknowledge that he would be unable to protect him.

By the time *Bend Sinister* was published in June 1947 Nabokov had already written another major story, 'Signs and Symbols', and begun the first chapters of his autobiography, originally entitled *Conclusive Evidence*, which was published in 1951. The following year, in preparation for his Cornell classes and prompted by an already substantial body of translated poetry, he began planning a literal translation of Pushkin's *Eugene Onegin*, a project that would absorb him for the next fifteen years. In 1950 he began another new novel, *A Kingdom By the Sea*, something he had been planning since

1947, but which over six years would evolve into his most famous book, the story of a paedophile, Humbert Humbert, and his nymphet, Lolita. Meanwhile, Nabokov was teaching three courses at Cornell, had written his last two short stories, 'The Vane Sisters' and 'Lance', taken up a visiting lectureship at Harvard, and begun writing what was to be his fourth English novel, *Pnin*, about an émigré teacher of Russian struggling to be taken seriously by his American campus colleagues.

Although Nabokov finished work on *Lolita* in December 1953, it was to take another two years to find a publisher – the Olympia Press in Paris – and a further three years before the book appeared in the United States. In the meantime, between November 1953 and November 1955, chapters One, Three, Four and Six of *Pnin* were published serially in the *New Yorker* with a final, seventh chapter completed that August. The entire novel was published in March 1957 to rave reviews and quickly went into a second printing. Nabokov was hailed as 'one of the subtlest, funniest, and most moving writers in the United States today'.[50]

Pnin spans just over four years in '"concurrent time" and more than half a century of retrospection'[51] in the life of its hero, during his last years as a teacher of Russian at Waindell College, New England. As in *Bend Sinister*, Nabokov deploys a circular framing structure. The novel opens as Pnin journeys to Cremona where he is to give a lecture. He mistakes his train, then takes the wrong bus, is stranded for a while in a small town where he almost dies of a heart attack, manages to hitch a lift and arrives just in time, endures another, faint seizure at the lectern, but nevertheless manages to deliver his lecture intact and with the correct script. As the story closes, a Waindell colleague, Jack Cockerell, is about to relate all this to Pnin's successor and the novel's narrator, Professor N–. 'Some people', N– declares, 'and I am one of them – hate happy ends. We feel cheated. Harm is the norm. Doom should not jam.' Pnin, however, proves that happy endings are

British cover of *Pnin*
by J. Faczynksi, 1957.

possible, no matter how extreme or frequent the disasters that plague him.

Pnin's character, like the round 'dome' of his bald head, his 'strong-man torso', 'heavy tortoise-shell reading glasses' and 'smoothly bulging' Russian 'potato nose', is robust, solid and determinedly self-sufficient. Before the narrative has even begun, he has already suffered four heart attacks, the loss of his family and his country, a loveless marriage and a painful divorce, and the tragic slaughter of his first love, Mira Belochkin, by the Nazis at Buchenwald. Sadness has been the single most reliably endur-ing aspect of his existence. 'Why not leave their private sorrows to people?' he asks. 'Is sorrow not . . . the only thing in the world people really possess?' Whether or not the final vision of a 'free' Pnin 'boldly' driving away from Waindell is an attempt on N–'s part to assuage his guilt for robbing him of his job or for being the 'dreadful inventor'[52] of Pnin's story is immaterial, for the reader is left with a sense of a man who has neither relinquished his dignity nor allowed his independence to be compromised.

Pnin is generally regarded as one of Nabokov's 'most accessible and straightforward' works,[53] but beneath its benign surface lies a far more complex structural, thematic and narrative design, 'built on a whole series' of interlinked and carefully balanced 'inner organic transitions'[54] that occur in a 'tightly controlled pattern in which external repetition is accompanied by internal transformation'.[55] *Pnin*'s seven chapters also offer the closest rendition of the image of a spiral contained in a circle – the 'colored spiral in a small ball of glass' – which Nabokov used to describe his life. The novel's central chapter, Four, serves as the pivotal, 'antithetic arc' which initiates the narrative's transformative development, its 'unwinding' as Nabokov would have called it,[56] and with it, the gradual liberation of his quietly tormented hero.

This transformative dynamic is initiated by the key figure of chapter Four, Victor Wind, the son of Pnin's ex-wife, Liza. Here Pnin and Victor meet for the first time. That they are profoundly connected despite the lack of a blood tie is first suggested when Liza describes Pnin as Victor's 'water father', as opposed to his actual, 'land' father.[57] Not only does this prefigure the description of a supremely majestic Pnin swimming in the Cooks' lake in chapter Five, but it also introduces one of the major thematic motifs of the novel. Throughout Nabokov's fiction, water is indicative of the presence of supernal realms and esoteric linkages and, through the reflective quality it also shares with glass, its power to alter perspective, to refract and transform not only the shape of objects, but colours too. This is particularly significant in terms of Victor's instant empathy with Pnin, and is made explicit in the description of his exceptional artistic gift, expressed in a particular fascination with light and shade:

At six, Victor already distinguished what so many adults never learn to see – the colours of shadows, the difference in tint between the shadow of an orange and that of a plum or an avocado pear.[58]

The metaphysical function of motifs of water and light in *Pnin* are set in relief by their role in a short story of 1951, 'The Vane Sisters', in which the spectral influence of two dead sisters is dramatized by dripping icicles, running water, shadows, reflections and shifting colours.[59] In *Pnin*, the dynamic of *ostranenie*, identified by Victor's art teacher as 'the "naturalization" of man-made things',[60] is concentrated in Victor's artistic vision, described at the very mid-point of chapter Four, which acts as the pivotal scene that drives the positive trajectory of the second half of the novel. In this same section the theme of the spiral is also asserted, and two of the novel's other major motifs – Cinderella and the squirrel – introduced and reconfigured, initiating a process that links them inextricably to the ethereal qualities of water, colour and light (the name of Victor's art teacher is also no coincidence):

> Among the many exhilarating things Lake taught was that the order of the solar spectrum is not a closed circle but a spiral of tints from cadmium red and oranges through a strontian yellow and a pale paradisal green to cobalt blues and violets, at which point the sequence does not grade into red again but passes into another spiral, which starts with a kind of lavender grey and goes on to Cinderella shades transcending human perception.[61]

The Cinderella motif recurs in chapter Six at Pnin's party, again directly associated with Victor, when the glass bowl he has given Pnin is remarked upon by one of Pnin's guests, who imagines 'Cinderella's glass shoes to be exactly of that greenish blue tint'.

Pnin proudly replies that Cinderella's slippers were in fact made of fur and not glass, and particularly 'Russian squirrel fur – *vair*, in French . . . from *veveritsa*, Slavic for a certain beautiful, pale, winter-squirrel fur, having a bluish, or . . . columbine shade'. The Cinderella theme both extends the notion of happy endings in the novel and is here explicitly connected to its squirrel motif. These animals, also known as 'shadow-tails', have been acting as elusive companions to Pnin throughout his life (he suffers, coincidentally, from a 'shadow behind the heart', a condition Nabokov was diagnosed with in 1952). Their pervasive, sinister presence – suggestive of dark, otherworldly spirits – is dispelled by their connection to Pnin's former love, Mira, whose surname is a diminutive of *belka*, the Russian for squirrel. Pnin is uneasily aware of the possible presence of 'a democracy of ghosts' who, he suspects, attend 'to the destinies of the quick',[62] but he is neither able nor wants to identify them, preferring the more tangible reassurance of such things as Victor's bowl. In Nabokov's original *New Yorker* version, the bowl not only represents the sovereign 'rich, round inner world' that he guards, but also eloquently completes the final circle of his story.[63]

Nabokov's punishing work schedule meant that the only time he had to concentrate on his writing was during vacations. The summers of 1951–3 were crucial in the composition of *Lolita*, and in the last of these, *Lolita* and *Pnin* overlapped. The Nabokovs would set off in their Oldsmobile in search of butterflies. When the weather was bad, Nabokov wrote, using the back seat of their car as his own 'private mobile studio', crucially free of 'noise' and 'drafts'.[64] Back in Ithaca, he documented the manners, behaviour and interests of adolescent girls. He read social and psychological studies, interviewed the principal of a local girls' school, noted the latest fashions, listed songs from jukeboxes, the names of famous singers and actors, jotted down lines from magazines, adverts, radio and film. He scoured the newspapers for details of sex crimes and murders, and even consulted gun manuals.

Nabokov writing in his car.

One story in particular caught his attention, that of Sally Horner, who in 1948 at the age of eleven was abducted by 50-year-old Frank La Salle. For nearly two years he made her his fugitive sex slave, until he eventually dumped her in a California motel.[65] Another, earlier story, however, more distinctly prefigures Nabokov's scenario. Lita Grey was the second wife of the silent comedy star Charlie Chaplin.[66] They first met in 1915 when she was only seven (Chaplin was 26), when 'a chance visit took Chaplin to Kitty's Come-On Inn where [Lita's] mother, Nana, was a waitress'.[67] Five years later, on the set of *The Kid*, Chaplin singled her out from a crowd of extras, creating the part of the Flirting Angel for her, and even commissioned a studio artist to paint her portrait 'in the manner of Sir Joshua Reynolds's "Age of Innocence"'.[68] Then in 1923, Chaplin cast her as his leading lady in *The Gold Rush*. Within a year she was pregnant. Threatened with charges of statutory rape Chaplin took Lita to Mexico and married her, commenting to reporters that 'this is better than penitentiary but it won't last'. In 1928 Lita filed for divorce on the grounds of serial infidelity and maltreatment. She claimed that

Lita Grey.

Chaplin had 'read banned books' to her and argued that 'all people do it' when she objected to his demands for oral sex, which she called an 'abnormal, against nature, perverted degenerate and indecent act'. Chaplin contended that he was simply 'like many other foolish men' and blamed Lita's mother for forcing her daughter on him. The divorce caused a huge scandal that threatened not only Chaplin's career but the business of five Hollywood studios. Lita was granted a settlement of $625,000, and in 1929 Chaplin's 'versatility and genius' was honoured by the Motion Picture Academy at their first Oscar awards ceremony.[69]

Lita Grey's real name was Lillita McMurray. Apart from the obvious similarities between the two heroines' first names, throughout Nabokov's narrative Lolita is also explicitly associated with the colour grey – as reflected in her 'great gray eyes'. She even dies in a fictitious Alaskan town called Gray Star, which Nabokov referred to as the 'capital town of the book'. Meanwhile, the ethereal implications of grey are magnified by a range of astral allusions – a 'gray star is one veiled by haze (Lolita's surname)', whilst the spell cast upon Humbert by Annabel Leigh, his lost 'Riviera love', is delineated by a 'haze of stars'.[70]

Lolita was finally published in the US in August 1958. Three years earlier Nabokov's 'timebomb'[71] had been rejected by five major publishers, who feared its controversial subject-matter would ruin them. Desperate, Nabokov asked his French literary agent to try to place it and in June 1955 a deal was struck with Maurice Girodias of Paris's Olympia Press. Although its list included some of the century's most celebrated authors – Samuel Beckett, Henry Miller and William Burroughs – the Press made most of its money from low-grade erotica. Unaware of this, Nabokov was happy to sign a contract and, in October 1955 5,000 copies were printed and distributed in 'two rather seedy pale olive-green paperback volumes'.[72] Because of the Press's reputation, *Lolita* initially made no impact at all, remaining in total obscurity until the British author, Graham Greene, listed it as one of the best novels of 1955 in the *Sunday Times*. Greene was subsequently to campaign for its UK publication, declaring that 'In England I may go to prison, but there couldn't be a better cause!'[73] His praise for the novel sparked a furious transatlantic controversy that raged, unabated, throughout 1956 and into 1957. Meanwhile, *Lolita* had become an underground sensation, a notorious work banned by the British and French authorities. With public curiosity rising to fever pitch, in June 1957 the *Anchor Review* printed a long extract, accompanied by an explanatory essay by Nabokov – 'On a Book Entitled *Lolita*' – and 'an endlessly long and boring critical introduction' by Columbia University's Fred Dupee. This was not simply an attempt to sanction the extract with reputable scholarship, but a deliberate strategy whereby the introduction would be 'so boring that the censors would not be able to get through it to get to the book itself'.[74] Its reception was universally positive, and just over a year later *Lolita* went on sale in American bookstores.

For a while Nabokov was unconcerned by the commotion *Lolita*'s publication generated. 'Occupied with a new story, and with the spreading of some 2,000 butterflies', he was 'serenely indifferent' to the fact that his novel had by its fourth day gone into a third printing.[75] Unable to ignore the clamour for long, he started a diary, 'Hurricane Lolita', to record the extraordinary phenomenon of this novel that might never have materialized had Véra not dissuaded him from burning an early draft in 1950.

The instantaneousness of *Lolita*'s impact was unprecedented. Within three weeks it had sold over 100,000 copies, and by September Nabokov had secured a prominent Hollywood agent, Irving 'Swifty' Lazar, whose client list included Humphrey Bogart, Cary Grant, Lauren Bacall, Gregory Peck, Cole Porter, Noel Coward, Ira Gershwin, Ernest Hemingway, Tennessee Williams and Truman Capote. Lazar brokered a $150,000 deal with James Harris and Stanley Kubrick for the film rights, including 15 per cent of the producers' rights. In the meantime, paperback rights were sold for $100,000. Nabokov was rapidly becoming a household name. *Lolita* had shot to the top of the *New York Times* bestseller list where it would stay for nearly a year and was a topic of daily comment in the press and on television, in jokes and cartoons. 'I've put off reading Lolita for six years,' quipped Groucho Marx, 'till she's 18.'

Despite the 'unbelievable success' of *Lolita*, Nabokov felt it 'ought to have happened 30 years ago'. Still, his psychic sensibilities confirmed that this was, in fact, the right time. When he saw the names of Harris and Kubrick on his Hollywood contract they broke a dream that he had had in 1916, shortly after the death of his Uncle Ruka, in which his uncle told him he would return as 'Harry and Kuvyrkin'.[76] Suddenly the mystery of the dream was solved, his destiny sealed, and the inheritance promised to him over 40 years before restored.

For Nabokov, *Lolita* 'was like the composition of a beautiful puzzle – its composition and its solution at the same time, since one is a mirror view of the other, depending on the way you look'.[77] In a letter to Edmund Wilson shortly after *Lolita*'s publication, he expressed dismay at Wilson's warning that his 'pure and austere work may be treated by some flippant critic as a pornographic stunt'. 'The danger is the more real to me,' Nabokov explained, 'since I realize that *even* you neither understand nor wish to understand the texture of this intricate and unusual production.'[78] Nabokov stood firm in the face of the controversy his novel generated, defending it as a 'serious work of art', his 'best book so far'[79] and insisting that, far from celebrating the monstrous perversion of a sexual predator, it was the tragic tale of a child's life destroyed. 'What is this evil deed I have committed?', he protested, 'Seducer, criminal – is this the word / for me who set the entire world a-dreaming / of my poor little girl?'[80]

Nevertheless, the sense of Lolita's tragedy is almost wholly subsumed by Humbert's capricious, elaborate and highly treacherous narrative. Although the apparent veracity of his 'confession' is undermined by evasiveness, ambivalence and ambiguity, the figure that emerges is that of 'a splendid sinner' who 'compels our admiration by the fineness and very excess of his wickedness'.[81] Humbert's fugitive world of cynicism, deception, contradiction, equivocation and delusion is offset by moments of disarming candour, admissions of acute self-loathing and bitter regret, but at no point do such aberrations diminish the intensity of his obsession or the urgency of his illicit romantic quest. At the same time, Humbert's highly allusive text creates 'complex juxtapositions' and 'ironic dismantlings', whilst the extent of its frame of reference – from medieval romance, fairy tales and gothic fantasy to shifting traditions in poetry and drama and twentieth-century preoccupations with film and popular music – offers both 'serious tributes' to and 'playful parodies' of some of the most renowned and equally obscure facets of Western art and culture.[82]

The foregrounded inter- and extra-textuality of Humbert's memoir is magnified by John Ray, Jr's Foreword which, in the paratextual tradition of the 'Gothic device of the posthumous manuscript from jail',[83] establishes Humbert's crime and details the fate of the story's protagonists. 'The caretakers of the various cemeteries involved report that no ghosts walk', Ray concludes.[84] Yet how far is his account any more reliable than Humbert's duplicitous narrative? Can we believe that 'no ghosts walk', and if Humbert's tale *is* haunted, who by? Annabel? Valeria? Charlotte? Quilty? Meanwhile, the self-reflexive aspect of J. R., Jr's name echoes Humbert Humbert's 'double rumble',[85] extending the all-pervasive theme of mirroring beyond the boundaries of Humbert's tale. Used as a means to express his acute self-consciousness, most dramatically in the sequence at the Enchanted Hunters hotel – 'There was a double bed, a mirror, a double bed in the mirror, a closet door with mirror, a bathroom door ditto, a blue-dark window, a reflected bed there, the same in the closet mirror, two chairs, a glass-topped table' – it also compounds Humbert's preoccupation with watching and being watched, his paranoid sense of living in 'a lighted house of glass'.[86] A further complicating factor is the question of whether the entire last section of the book – from when Humbert receives Lolita's letter at the end of chapter 27 – actually happens. This is initiated by a glaring discrepancy in dates that cancels out the critical scenes at Coalmont and Pavor Manor, and undermines the central premise of Humbert's narrative.[87] *Lolita*, however, offers no solutions. By constructing a narrative of so many layers, Humbert attempts to deny the presence of any perspective other than his own, and yet it is punctured by discreet voids, or fissures, that offer brief, tantalizing glimpses of a remote yet distinct universe uncorrupted by his solipsistic, self-serving, ulterior vision. The reader may be able to determine these 'secret points, the subliminal co-ordinates by means of which the book is plotted',[88] but they remain exasperatingly and defiantly oblique. 'Art is difficult',[89] Nabokov contended, and the difficulty of *Lolita* challenges even the most discerning, meticulous and sceptical reader.

The figure of Edgar Allan Poe casts a long shadow across Humbert's tale, his song of doomed childhood romance, 'Annabel Lee', providing Humbert with an evocative subtext for the loss of his Riviera love and a compelling pretext for his quest to recover her. Along with other distinguished names in Western culture, most prominently Dante and Petrarch, Poe conveniently serves, in both his art and his life, to support Humbert's efforts to legitimize and romanticize his actions.[90] At the same time, there exists behind this foregrounded context a network of implicit allusions to a series of more obscure, yet equally telling figures, contained in seemingly insignificant details.

Of all the names from Western European art Humbert cites, he selects for special attention a late nineteenth-century British artist. Aubrey Beardsley was a decadent with 'a morbid sexual obsession',[91] famous for his darkly grotesque, perversely erotic illustrations of works by Poe and Wilde. Humbert and Lolita settle in Beardsley after their year on the road, and Aubrey is linked with the forces of fate, which Humbert makes tangible through personification and then through identification, citing 'that devil of mine' as complicit in his devious schemes,[92] and yet this same Aubrey

McFate is also listed as one of Lolita's Ramsdale classmates. Whilst Beardsley seems an ideal model for Humbert, his work demonstrating 'lasciviousness as Humbert would have liked us to see it: camouflaged by the exuberance of decadent art',[93] his name randomly appears as one of the pseudonyms that Quilty leaves in twenty of the 342 hotel registers that Humbert scours during his 'cryptogrammic paper chase'.[94] Quilty's adoption of the name signals the extent to which he has assumed control, but also the degree to which Humbert's perception of the scenario is distorted by paranoia. Whereas before he was blind to the presence of his nemesis, now he sees him everywhere. The course of the name's recurrence across the narrative exemplifies the way in which repetition, rather than establishing a stable, developing pattern of meaning and association, generates instability and inconsistency. This latent unpredictability is at once expressive of Humbert's artful depiction of events, his vacillating stance and his precarious grip on actuality.

Meanwhile, the *commedia dell'arte* heroine, Columbine, also makes an appearance. Although she is never directly associated with Lolita, Humbert establishes a connection by bringing her a book called *Clowns and Columbines* when she is in hospital in Elphinstone. The name subsequently recurs when he is describing Rita, the woman he picks up in a bar 'somewhere between Montreal and New York' and abandons, just as casually, two years later. 'The oddly prepubescent curve of her back, her ricey skin, her slow languorous columbine kisses kept me from mischief',[95] he claims. In the *commedia dell'arte* tradition, the lovely and fickle Columbine (the flower, known as the herb of Venus, is emblematic of folly and deserted love) is unable to resist Harlequin and abandons Pierrot, her dreamy, love-struck clown. In this scenario, Humbert would cast himself as Pierrot and Quilty Harlequin, but Humbert also shares Harlequin's 'duality of charm and danger, artistry and artiness, ostentation and concealment'.[96] By assuming both roles, Humbert disrupts the *commedia dell'arte*'s classic love triangle and fractures the rivalry between Pierrot and Harlequin, which in turn undermines his own struggle against Quilty. At the same time, by never fully passing Harlequin's mask to Quilty, Humbert curiously aligns himself with his arch rival, blurring the distinctions between them.

Whilst Humbert manipulates the *commedia dell'arte* allusions to his own ends, the harlequin theme intriguingly coalesces with references to Aubrey Beardsley. Beardsley was idolized by the Russian pre-Revolutionary 'World of Art' movement, to which Nabokov's parents were closely connected through their 'many acquaintances who painted and danced and made music'.[97] His illustrations for Ernest Dowson's play, *The Pierrot of the Minute*, were highly influential in Russia, as was the play itself, and his

Illustration for the Ballets Russes production, *Carnaval*, St Petersburg, 1910 (left to right: Pierrot, Columbine, Harlequin).

Frontispiece from *The Pierrot of the Minute* by Aubrey Beardsley.

work was featured in the Symbolist journal, *Vesy* (*The Scales*), and the first numbers of Diaghilev's 'World of Art' magazine. Beardsley's style complemented the harlequinade tradition of artifice and the grotesque, the fantastic and the absurd which informed contemporary poetry, art and drama, and particularly the subversive and transformative work of avant-garde theatre director, Vsevelod Meyerhol´d. Meyerhol´d's emphasis on 'the demonic in its deepest irony; the tragicomic in the quotidian; a striving for unbelievable conventions; mysterious intimations' and 'dissonance elevated to the harmoniously beautiful',[98] anticipates Nabokov's principle of spectacular invention, voiced by Vadim's aunt in his last complete novel:

Look at the harlequins! Trees are harlequins, words are harlequins. So are situations and sums. Put two things together – jokes, images – and you get a triple harlequin. Come on! Play! Invent the world! Invent reality![99]

Humbert does precisely this, whilst cynically despairing that he has 'only words to play with'.[100]

The Columbine theme can also be pursued beyond *Lolita* where it coincides with the 'beautiful, pale, winter-squirrel fur' of Pnin's Cinderella slipper. The ethereal, otherworldly qualities of its 'bluish', 'columbine shade'[101] extend still further to the transcendent grey of Lake's solar spectrum. These associations imply that Lolita is more than the nymphet that Humbert sees, and perhaps belongs elsewhere, a suggestion further enforced by the novel's butterfly allusions initiated, surprisingly, by Quilty.

When Humbert confronts Quilty at Pavor Manor with a poem and a gun – the poem a crude parody of T. S. Eliot's 'Ash Wednesday' and the gun a prop in his unfulfilled revenge scenario – Quilty attempts to distract him by prattling stream-of-consciousness nonsense. 'I am a playwright', he says, 'I have been called the American Maeterlinck. Maeterlinck–Schmetterling, says I.' Nabokov later commented that this was 'the most important phrase in the chapter'. Quilty refers to himself as a playwright in the guise of Maurice Maeterlinck who, 'in an effort to communicate the mysteries of man's inner life and his relation to the universe . . . created a theater of stasis, rich in atmosphere and short in action'. Humbert has already described Quilty's 'fancy' play, *The Enchanted Hunters*, as 'pretty dismal', 'with echoes of Lenormand and Maeterlinck and various quiet British dreamers'.[102] But Maeterlinck also wrote extensively on parallel worlds and the fourth dimension,[103] concepts central to Nabokov's metaphysics, whilst his opinions on tragic theatre closely parallel Nabokov's fictional imperative:

Humbert (James Mason, right) confronts Quilty (Peter Sellers, left) with a gun and a poem. *Lolita*, dir. Stanley Kubrick, 1962.

the only words that count . . . are those that at first seemed useless, for it is therein that the essence lies. Side by side with the necessary dialogue will you almost always find another dialogue that seems superfluous; but examine it carefully, and it will be borne home to you that this is the only one that the soul can listen to profoundly, for here alone is it the soul that is being addressed.[104]

Humbert aligns Maeterlinck with 'various quiet British dreamers', but his dismissive intent is again subverted by his generalized evocation of the Edwardian writers Nabokov so admired – Brooke, Housman, Wells and de la Mare. This is also not the first occurrence of Schmetterling, the German word for butterfly. It appears as one of Quilty's many hotel register aliases, combined with an anglicized version of Maeterlinck's first name, 'Morris'.[105] The associations of Quilty with butterflies connects him, obliquely, with Lolita, who is designated a nymphet by her 'faint musky fragrance',[106] a scent reminiscent of the 'musk and vanilla' odour of butterflies.[107] It is ironic that, having been indifferent to moths, butterflies and bugs throughout his tale, it is only on his way to Pavor Manor that Humbert finally notices these creatures as they fly into the light of his headlamps – 'like derelict snowflakes, moths drifted out of the blackness into my probing aura'.[108] Here they are directly juxtaposed with the ephemera of Lolita's past – 'There was still a three-year-old bobby pin of hers in the depths of the glove compartment. There was still that stream of pale moths siphoned out of the night by my headlights' – now delicately evocative of a lost, remote world. Even flies, once 'lousy' and 'creeping', become expressive of Humbert's remorse, transformed into the 'beautiful bright-green flies' that cluster on the blood and marrow of his tale.[109]

Humbert's cynical dismissal of Quilty's exotic drama is critical in that it draws the reader's attention away from what seems to be merely a burlesque parody of his tale but which in fact 'offers a "message" that can be taken seriously as a commentary on the progression of the entire novel' – 'that mirage and reality merge in love'. Humbert may scoff, but it is precisely this transformation that he experiences and celebrates when finally confronted by the 'washed-out gray eyes' of a 'strangely-spectacled', 'pale and polluted'[110] Dolly Schiller:

> I looked and looked at her, and knew as clearly as I know I am to die, that I loved her more than anything I had ever seen or imagined on earth, or hoped for anywhere else.[111]

Humbert's mistake is to ignore the seemingly inconsequential details of Lolita's universe for, in Nabokov's world, 'only myopia condones the blurry generalization of ignorance'.[112] Humbert's deranged mind and his unreliable memory – 'a sort of retrospective imagination which feeds the analytic faculty with boundless alternatives and . . . causes a visualized route to fork and re-fork without end in the maddeningly complex prospect of my past'[113] – handicap him, fatally. Whereas the 'forces of imagination remain steadfastly on Smurov's side', Humbert's compromised vision denies him the potential for 'goodness'. His mission, to 'fix once for all the perilous magic of nymphets',[114] to ensnare an innately transient being, is futile, his 'quest for Arcadia, for the past, for the unattainable itself'[115] a miserable parody of the triumph over time that Nabokov achieves in art through the combined forces of memory and the imagination. Humbert claims to be a poet, and yet his creative sensibility is far removed from the 'immemorial urge' of the Nabokovian poet who tries 'to express [his] position in regard to the universe embraced by consciousness' through a process of 'cosmic synchronisation'. Feeling 'everything that happens in one point in time', he indiscriminately assimilates the diverse and multifarious elements of his world to form 'an instantaneous and transparent organism of events' of which he is 'the nucleus'.[116] The closest Humbert comes to sensing synchronous events is when, sitting in his upstairs room in Charlotte's house, he likens himself to an 'inflated pale' spider in the 'middle of a luminous web', jerking its silken strands in a futile effort to determine Lolita's whereabouts.[117] Incapable of achieving true art, his memoir serves merely as a 'refuge' which he condemns Lolita to share with him – 'Imagine me', he pleads, 'I shall not exist if you do not imagine me.'[118] Humbert's perception of the eternity granted by art is, essentially, the only 'kind of immortality that the sinner can share with his victim, which leave[s] open the possibility' – implied all along – 'that Lolita occupies another space altogether'.[119]

With *Lolita*, Nabokov reasserted the 'dream of pure invention'[120] that had inspired the major creative departure of *King, Queen, Knave*. *Lolita*'s theme, he said, was 'so distant, so remote, from my own emotional life that it gave me a special pleasure to use my combinational talent to make it real'.[121] Despite the difficulty of this 'enormous, mysterious, heartbreaking novel' that had taken 'five years of monstrous misgivings and diabolical labors',[122] Nabokov had produced a work of extraordinary ingenuity and integrity. In the words of Robert Louis Stevenson, on whom Nabokov lectured at Cornell, the 'web' and 'pattern' of *Lolita* is 'at once sensuous and logical, an elegant and pregnant texture: That is style, that is the foundation of the art of literature'.[123]

6

World Fame:
Hollywood and Switzerland, 1958–68

Nobody can decide if I am a middle-aged American writer or an old
Russian writer – or an ageless international freak.[1]

In September 1958, Nabokov returned to Cornell, opening his
lecture on Jane Austen's *Mansfield Park* with the instruction, 'OMIT
IDIOTIC INTRODUCTION!!!!!'.[2] He also brought with him his new
English versions of Lermontov's *A Hero of Our Time* and the
medieval Russian epic *The Song of Igor's Campaign*.[3] By mid-term
he was struggling to combine his teaching with the demands of
publishers, promoters, lawyers and the press, and requested a year's
sabbatical. He gave his last lectures in January 1959 and in April
headed West once again, spending two months hunting butterflies
in Arizona, where he was joined by a *Sports Illustrated* reporter,[4]
before finally heading to Los Angeles to meet with James Harris and
Stanley Kubrick. They were keen that Nabokov write the screenplay
for their film, but he did not agree with the changes they proposed
and at the end of July headed back to New York, leaving them to find
another writer. By the autumn Nabokov had resigned from Cornell
and was preparing to leave for Europe. He wanted to visit his sister,
Elena, in Geneva, and Dmitri, who was now training as an opera
singer, needed to be settled with a new teacher in Milan. There
were also two major launch events planned for *Lolita* in Paris and
London, and negotiations for an important Italian contract to be
finalized. Meanwhile, Nabokov was hoping to find a quiet retreat

where he could write undisturbed – he had already begun the essay that would become Van Veen's 'Texture of Time', the philosophical treatise at the heart of *Ada*, and was anxious to focus on the ideas inspired by his stay at 880 Highland Road.

On 5 November, the eve of *Lolita*'s British publication, the Nabokovs attended a lavish party at the Ritz Hotel in London, hosted by Weidenfeld and Nicolson. Although Nabokov 'claimed to be enjoying himself tremendously', he was never comfortable in crowds. One onlooker commented that he 'wore the bemused air of a man who wasn't quite sure what the party was all about'.[5] When the evening began, no one knew whether or not the British government would prosecute, but at the last minute, news came through that they were to take no action. *Lolita* was published, as scheduled, the next day, and the Nabokovs were once again besieged by the press, such that Véra remarked, 'Lolita is every inch of a *cause célèbre*.'[6]

A few weeks later, Nabokov received a telegram from Kubrick asking if he would reconsider his decision regarding the screenplay. Nabokov was now more amenable to the idea, but only if he could be given absolute freedom to write without interference. Kubrick agreed. By the end of January 1960 Irving Lazar had secured a $40,000 deal for the screenplay, with a further $35,000 for a sole on-screen credit. The Nabokovs arrived in Los Angeles at the beginning of March and Lazar immediately set about introducing them to a select crowd that included John Huston, David O. Selznick and Ira Gershwin. Of all the people they met, Nabokov was particularly impressed by Billy Wilder, whom he described as a 'worldly, cultivated man'.[7] He found Marilyn Monroe delightful – 'she was gloriously pretty, all bosom and rose'[8] – but failed to recognize John Wayne. When he asked what he did for a living, Wayne modestly replied, 'I'm in pictures'.[9]

Véra and Vladimir soon abandoned the Hollywood social scene and withdrew to their rented house on Mandeville Canyon Road – a long, winding, wooded lane off Sunset Boulevard that backed onto the wild ridges of the Santa Monica mountains, where Nabokov 'had seclusion and freedom, and a canyon full of butterflies'.[10] He 'worked with zest, composing mentally every morning from eight to noon while butterfly hunting in the hot hills'. After 'a leisurely lunch' he

> would spend another four-hour span in a lawn chair, among the roses and mockingbirds, using lined index cards and a Black-wing pencil, for copying and recopying, rubbing out and writing anew, the scenes [he] had imagined in the morning.[11]

'The screenplay became poetry', he remarked, 'which was my original purpose.'[12] Nabokov's completed script ran to 400 pages. Kubrick was dismayed, saying that it was 'too unwieldy, contained too many unnecessary episodes, and would take about seven hours to run'.[13] On receiving a drastically cut version, Kubrick told Nabokov that his was 'the best screenplay ever written in Hollywood', but Harris subsequently admitted that Nabokov's 'huge' script was 'unfilmable': 'You couldn't make it. You couldn't even *lift* it.'[14] At the film's premiere in 1962, Nabokov was disappointed to see that 'only ragged odds and ends of [his] script' had been used, but hailed Kubrick as 'a great director', calling 'his *Lolita*' 'a first-rate film with magnificent actors'.[15] Although Kubrick substantially rewrote Nabokov's screenplay he retained several scenes that worked cinematically – the Ramsdale High School summer dance, Humbert and Lolita on the road and the final sequence at the Schillers' house. Kubrick demonstrated an ingenious ability to render distinctive Nabokovian themes and motifs, whilst skilfully balancing key dynamics of comedy, irony and pathos.[16] The film

Nabokov at Mandeville Canyon Road, Los Angeles, 1960.

Poster for Kubrick's *Lolita*, 1962.

also featured some inspired set-pieces, two of which – the opening confrontation at Pavor Manor played across a ping-pong table, and Humbert drunk in the bathtub following Charlotte's accident – Nabokov singled out as 'delightful'.[17] Despite Kubrick's major rewrite, Nabokov retained sole credit for the screenplay and in 1963 was nominated for an Oscar.

In November 1960 the Nabokovs headed back to Europe, settling in Nice, where Vladimir was finally able to concentrate on his new book. *Pale Fire* was to consist of a 999-line poem, written by a fictional poet, John Shade, accompanied by a foreword, commentary and index by its psychotic editor Charles Kinbote – alias Charles II of Zembla, alias V. Botkin. The day Shade completes his 999th line (the planned penultimate line of his poem), he is shot by Jack Grey, an escaped convict who has mistaken him for his neighbour, Judge Goldsworth. Kinbote, however, believes that *he* was the intended target, and that the assassin is Jakob Gradus, a revolutionary 'Shadow' on a regicidal mission from Zembla.

Stanley Kubrick draws a pair of heart-shaped sunglasses under the title 'Lolita' on the end of a prop bomb on the set of *Dr Strangelove* (1964).

Nabokov finished work on the poem – 'the hardest stuff I ever had to compose'[18] – in February 1961, and over the spring and summer he and Véra made several trips to Italy to see Dmitri sing a series of principal operatic roles. Dmitri's 'great gifts, the rare beauty of his bass, and the promise of a splendid career' affected Nabokov 'deeply', and yet he had 'no ear for music'. He deplored 'bitterly' that he was unable to 'follow the sequence and relationship of sounds' for any longer than a few minutes, but 'what could [he] do if ear and brain refuse[d] to cooperate?'[19] Returning to Switzerland in the autumn, the Nabokovs moved into a suite of rooms on the third floor of the sumptuous Montreux Palace Hotel, overlooking Lake Geneva. Here, in the hotel's 'enchanting and inspiring gardens',[20] Vladimir was finally able to concentrate on Kinbote's commentary.

Pale Fire was 'conceived as a sort of self-irony',[21] its '*Theme*' inspired by Nabokov's work on Pushkin's *Eugene Onegin* – 'a novel, a life, a love – which is only the elaborate commentary to a gradually evolved short poem.'[22] *Onegin* had more than lived up to Nabokov's initial gargantuan vision:

> I want translations with copious footnotes, footnotes reaching up like skyscrapers to the top of this or that page so as to leave only the gleam of one textual line between commentary and

Nabokov writing on the terrace of the Montreux Palace Hotel.

eternity . . . And when my *Onegin* is ready, it will either conform exactly to my vision or not appear at all.[23]

Soon, Nabokov's 'burgeoning commentary' began to 'over-shadow the poem itself', its focus shifting 'from the text to the appendage, from the presumed center to the periphery'.[24] In *Pale Fire*, Kinbote's commentary overwhelms the poem it claims to annotate to a point of near obliteration, despite his assertion of having 'no desire to twist and batter an unambiguous *apparatus criticus* into the monstrous semblance of a novel'.[25] Shade's poem 'gradually disappears under the weight of [Kinbote's] commentary, as the true subject of the discourse emerges – the Critic himself, or Nothing'.[26]

Pale Fire stands as the most vaunted example of Nabokov's creative strategy – 'deceit, to the point of diabolism, and originality, verging upon the grotesque'.[27] This dynamic of deceit draws the reader into a process of oblique discovery, in an 'abundance of insidious tries' and 'false trails'[28] that are at once frustratingly opaque and astonishingly revelationary. At the same time, the novel sustains an unrelieved tension, generated by unresolved ambivalence and ambiguity, that realizes Nabokov's perception of the elusiveness of reality:

> You can never get nearer and nearer, so to speak, to reality; but you never get near enough because reality is an infinite succession of steps, levels of perception, false bottoms, and hence unquenchable, unattainable.[29]

Whilst the reader enters into a futile pursuit of the novel's fugitive realities, its protagonists seek to assert meaning, order and consequence in a world that defies understanding or control. The 'reality' of Shade's poem is overlain by Kinbote's exotic, quixotic commentary, much in the same way that Cincinnatus C.'s actuality is subsumed by a surreal yet convincingly palpable world. '"Reality"',

Kinbote argues, from a recognizably Nabokovian standpoint, 'is neither the subject nor the object of true art which creates its own special reality having nothing to do with the average "reality" perceived by the communal eye.'[30] The 'average reality' of the novel is the frame upon which Kinbote superimposes his 'special reality', peopled by the royals and revolutionaries of a 'distant northern land', the fantastical kingdom of Zembla, 'a land of reflections, of "resemblers"'.[31] No matter how compelling Kinbote's evocation of this alternative reality may be, as Véra Nabokov insisted, 'nobody knows, nobody should know – even Kinbote hardly knows – if Zembla really exists'.[32] Meanwhile, Shade attempts, in his poem, to ascertain a 'web of sense', a 'correlated pattern' in what initially seems to be the 'topsy-turvical coincidence' of life,[33] and yet he remains blind to the significant details embedded in the very work of art that he has created. Ironically, it is the insane impostor, Kinbote, who seems to possess the attributes of a true Nabokovian artist:

> I can do what only a true artist can do – pounce upon the forgotten butterfly of revelation, wean myself abruptly from the habit of things, see the web of the world, and the warp and the weft of that web[34]

but the reader knows that he, too, is fatally deluded.

In a further parody of his annotator's role in *Onegin*, Nabokov wove into the novel's 'fine fabric of deceit'[35] a dense network of literary allusions, ranging from folk legends, myths and fairy tales, to the English satirists Alexander Pope and Jonathan Swift – in whose *Battle of the Books*, for example, '"a malignant Deity, call'd *Criticism*" lives on a mountain in Nova Zembla'[36] – nineteenth-century Gothic Romanticism and twentieth-century European Modernism. Shade's poem explicitly emulates the poetry of Pope and Wordsworth, but also the style of his immediate contemporaries, Robert Frost and

T. S. Eliot, whilst invoking the shadows of Shakespeare's *Richard III* and *Henry IV, Part I*, and in its title, the pale fires of *Timon of Athens* and *Hamlet*.[37]

Although it is implied that Kinbote's 'pale fire' is the reflected glory he assumes through his editorship of Shade's poem, 'the poem itself' could equally be

> the pale fire (or the shadow cast by Pope and others), and the commentary (which is, after all, the bulk of the novel given us by Nabokov) the greater artistic blaze that quite puts the poet in the shade. . . . Kinbote might indeed be clinically a '*luna*tic' (and "arrant thief" like the *moon*), but – or therefore – possessed of a more divine poetic furor than Shade.[38]

Equally, the 'uneffectual fire' of the glow-worm that pales in Elsinore's dawn light and heralds the vanishing of King Hamlet's Ghost alludes to themes of death, loss and revenge enacted by Hazel, Shade and Gradus, respectively, as well as the supernatural, dramatized by the visitations of Shade's Aunt Maud in the form of a poltergeist.

The Shakespearean subtext is also key in initiating the novel's diabolical/supernatural/fatidic/absurd patterns of threes. King Hamlet's Ghost bids his son a triple farewell – 'Adieu, adieu, adieu. Remember me' – whilst *Timon* has three marauders – the moon, the sun and the sea. Kinbote's identity is threefold – he is at once Charles Xavier Vseslav, the last King of Zembla; Charles Kinbote, Shade's editor; and Botkin, Professor of Russian at Wordsmith College. One of the three heraldic characters on Kinbote's royal coat-of-arms is a bird called a '*sampel*' or 'silktail', similar to the waxwing that opens Shade's poem, its 'interesting association' only 'belatedly realized' (the waxwing's Latin name means 'silk-tail'),[39] whilst the trio of Zemblan misprints Kinbote cites reflect his triple personality – *korona* (crown = King Charles);

vorona (cow = Botkin); *korova* (crow = Kinbote).[40] Intriguingly, the pattern extends beyond Kinbote to Hazel, who spends three nights in a haunted barn. As Kinbote points out, 'There are always "three nights" in fairy tales, and in this sad fairy tale there was a third one too.'[41] The three *atalantas* – 'the Butterfly of Doom'[42] – embedded in the garbled spectral message she deciphers – presumably from Aunt Maud – anticipate Shade's death and Hazel's metamorphosed presence at the scene.[43] When abandoned by her blind date, Hazel becomes the third wheel of her group and leaves, humiliated. She drowns herself in one of three 'conjoined lakes' – Omega – at 'Lochan Neck' where skaters cross from Exe to Wye.[44]

Kinbote, appropriately, like his multi-faceted predecessor Smurov, chooses 'the irrational, the illogical' and 'the inexplicable' over 'the world of the matter-of-fact' to assert his own fabulous and highly comical fantasy – the creation of a fabricated persona impersonating an imaginary king. Although it may be driven by insanity, it is still an inspired achievement and this, along with the surprising sensitivity, empathy and insight Kinbote demonstrates, particularly towards Hazel and Disa – Duchess of Payn, Charles's 'lovely, pale, melancholy Queen' – deflates his cast as a 'monstrous parasite of a genius', or a paranoid megalomaniac. At the same time, Kinbote's bizarre humanity sets Shade's self-absorbed myopia in stark relief. Shade's poem focuses, in equal measure, on his mundane, everyday existence, the processes of his art and his preoccupation with his own mortality, his verse vacillating between flashes of profound insight and ponderous banality. That he should devote less than half of the second of four cantos to the suicide of his daughter suggests that this was a child who figured in his life as an awkward, confusing disruption, a 'difficult, morose' 'darling', to be pitied, but never truly celebrated.[45]

Shade's anguished attempts to 'explore and fight' death – 'the foul, the inadmissible abyss'[46] – echo Nabokov's precarious vision of himself 'rock[ing] above' the 'abyss' of eternity, and his 'colossal efforts to distinguish the faintest glimmers in the impersonal darkness on both sides of my life'.[47] For Shade, to die is to be 'tossed / Into a boundless void, your bearings lost, / Your spirit stripped and utterly alone, / Your task unfinished, your despair unknown'.[48] Hazel's death simply confirms his scepticism:

> . . . no self-styled
> Spirit would touch a keyboard of dry wood
> To rap out her pet name; no phantom would
> Rise gracefully to welcome you and me
> In the dark garden, near the shagbark tree.[49]

Yet Hazel's phantom rises exactly as Shade imagines, and on the day he dies, as a 'magnificent, velvet-and-flame creature', the Red Admiral butterfly, or *Vanessa atalanta*, which flashes briefly in the evening sun before dissolving into the shadows.

Shade 'lacks the artist's gift of making connections'. He fails to notice the portent of his daughter's invocation of T. S. Eliot's *Four Quartets*, or a fateful allusion to Pushkin contained in his own work.[50] Kinbote, on the other hand, demonstrates a poetic and psychic sensibility that enables him to be

> enriched with an indescribable amazement as if informed that fireflies were making decodable signals on behalf of stranded spirits, or that a bat was writing a legible tale of torture in the bruised and branded sky.[51]

Kinbote's 'decodable signals', however, only add to the dizzying effect of *Pale Fire*'s accumulation of mirrors and reflections, shadows and doubles, anagrams, puns, palindromes, numerical and alphabetic sequences. Textual confusion is compounded by shifts in narrative voice which undermine the autonomy of the novel's extant authors, Shade and Kinbote, indicating another, involute authorial dynamic that could be generated by either Botkin or Nabokov.

Pale Fire's elusive quality is initiated by the very opening lines of Shade's poem – 'I was the shadow of the waxwing slain / By the false azure in the windowpane'.[52] The image introduces central themes of misapprehension, deception and optical illusion, and is itself highly ambiguous. Can it be read, simply, as a romantic analogy of Shade's demise, rendering him a victim, like the waxwing, of a misapprehension, in his case, mistaken identity? Yet it is not clear whether it is the bird or the shadow that dies – shade and shadow are congruous, after all – whilst Kinbote could equally be identified as the waxwing. The implication is that the bird symbolizes Shade, which would identify it as a Cedar Waxwing, common to an Appalachian garden, and yet the provenance of its cousin, the Bohemian Waxwing, is Kinbote/Botkin's domain – the northern regions of Scandinavia and Russia, extending as far east as Kamchatka, where Nabokov's great grandfather was an explorer, incorporating the archipelago Novaya Zemlya, where a river was named after him. If Shade is the shadow, and Kinbote the waxwing, then this reinforces the notion of Shade as a 'pale fire' to Kinbote's bright flame. The lines' past-tense cast suggests that Shade is already dead when he begins his poem – a possibility since, according to Kinbote, 'our shadows still walk without us'[53] – but is it more likely that this is Kinbote's work? Kinbote asserts, emphatically, that the manuscript 'contains not one gappy line, not one doubtful reading', and yet other experts – the Shadeans – insist that it is 'disjointed' and far from definitive. Has Kinbote, therefore, interfered not only with the poem's content, but its form and its order? He is confident that Shade's 1,000th line would have been a repetition of its first, completing the 'symmetry of the structure with its two identical central parts, solid and ample, forming together with the shorter flanks twin images of five hundred verses each'.[54] Kinbote's description evokes the wings of a butterfly and with it, his preoccupation with mimetic patterning, and yet the image is fraudulent, its eloquence serving to distract the reader's attention away from the fundamental questions it raises. Where and what are these 'two identical central parts' and how is the extant poem in any way symmetrical or twinned, other than in the projected repetition of its first and last lines? There are no obvious solutions. *Pale Fire* is 'an infernal machine',[55] inscrutable, contradictory, illusory, a subversive embodiment of Fyodor Godunov-Cherdyntsev's anti-revelation, whereby 'everything had acquired sense and at the same time everything was concealed'.[56]

Pale Fire's positive imagery, however, once apprehended, takes the reader in a different direction. The seemingly closed and dia-bolical threes at once combine with the novel's predominant reflective motifs to produce a 'fantastic mirror', a 'triptych of bot-tomless light' that transforms its subjects into endlessly repeating and expanding magical incarnations, 'diminishing into the limpid distance'.[57] Meanwhile, repetitions of the number eight, represen-tative of infinity, are suggested by lemniscates and ampersands, which figure most overtly in connection with the Zemblan actress, Iris Acht – whose legacy assists the King's escape – and more dis-creetly in the tracks of bicycle tyres or discarded rubber bands. They even take the shape of the lake – Omega – in which Hazel drowns (omega being the Greek number 800). Alongside these figures, the recurrence of the colour azure, contained in the open-ing lines of Shade's poem, signals the palpable presence of the otherworld. In *Invitation to a Beheading*, Cincinnatus C, 'envious of poets', dreams of being able to 'speed along a page and, right from the page, where only a shadow continues to run, to take off into the blue'.[58] This same potential for transcendence is evoked in the final vision of Shade lying on his back, 'with open dead eyes directed up at the sunny evening azure'.[59] Whilst his body, his shadow, remains earth-bound, his spirit flies on 'in the reflected sky'.[60]

This vision recurs in Nabokov's description, in *Speak, Memory*, of his father's transition, in death, into the sky's 'cobalt blue' (one of the 'spiral of tints' of his solar spectrum). As a child, Nabokov would often witness his father's subjection to a peasant ritual of thanks, which involved being 'rocked and tossed' by a 'score or so of strong arms':

> there he would be, on his last and loftiest flight, reclining as if for good, against the cobalt blue of the summer noon, like one of those paradisiac personages who comfortably soar, with such a wealth of folds in their garments, on the vaulted ceiling of a church while below, one by one, the wax tapers in mortal hands light up to make a swarm of minute flames in the mist of incense, and the priest chants the eternal repose, and funeral lilies conceal the face of whoever lies there, among the swimming lights, in the open coffin.[61]

In life and in death, V. D. Nabokov triumphs over both space and time. The vision of his floating body both anticipates and mirrors the ultimate transcendence of his spirit. The barriers between the material and metaphysical worlds dissolve – past, present and future are negated and layers of time compress into a single unit. Nabokov perceived time as a magic carpet, which he could fold 'in such a way as to superimpose one part of the pattern upon the other'.[62] Here, the spectacle of his father gloriously reclining in the sky is folded over the vision of soaring figures on a church ceiling, which is folded again over the image of a man lying in his coffin staring, like Shade, up into an infinite sky (the implied emotion in the 'swimming lights' identifies the man as Nabokov's father).[63] All three aspects, whilst remaining distinct, are inextricably linked by the layers of patterning they comprise, merging together to become a single time, space and death-defying entity.

Nabokov made two trips to America in 1962 and 1964 – for the premiere of Kubrick's *Lolita*, and the launch of his *Eugene Onegin* – but, despite his intentions, was never to return for good. In September 1962, Vladimir and Véra moved to an apartment on the top floor of the Montreux Palace Hotel, still overlooking the lake, which was to become their first and last permanent home. Hotel life suited Nabokov perfectly – it 'confirms me in my favorite habit', he said, 'the habit of freedom'. It also 'eliminate[d] the nuisance of private ownership'.[64] In Europe and America, the Nabokovs had become accustomed to meagre living. Endless relocation made it impossible for them to accumulate much in the way of possessions, but this proved of little concern since, as Nabokov explained, 'in my opulent childhood I was taught to regard with amused contempt any too-earnest attachment to material wealth'.[65] All he required was the use of a bathtub, a stock of pencils with rubbers on the end, and a butterfly net. His response

Vladimir and Véra by the pool at the Montreux Palace Hotel, 1966.

Vladimir and Dmitri, 1968.

to the immense sums of money his work began to generate after *Lolita* was one of modest surprise – 'Writing has always been for me a blend of dejection and high spirits, a torture and a pastime – but I never expected it to be a source of income.'[66] Over the next decade he was to amass a small fortune in film and publishing deals. In 1964, the *New Yorker* paid over £10,000 to serialize *The Defense* across two issues and *Playboy* $8,000 for *The Eye*. In 1967 Nabokov received a $250,000 advance on an eleven-book deal from McGraw-Hill and in 1968 and 1969 Hollywood bought the film rights to *King, Queen, Knave* and *Ada* for $100,000 and $500,000 respectively.

In June 1962, following the publication of *Pale Fire* in April and to mark the opening of Kubrick's *Lolita*, Nabokov made the cover of *Newsweek*. In July the BBC arrived in Montreux to film him. By the mid-1960s, media interest was so intense that on return from one summer vacation Nabokov was greeted by a 'madhouse of interviews, photographers, publishers . . . and TV'.[67] He didn't enjoy being interviewed – 'Nobody should ask me to submit to an interview if by "interview" a chat between two normal human beings is implied'[68] – insisting that questions be sent to him in advance and that only his proofed replies could be published. Sometimes 'great trouble was taken to achieve the illusion of a spontaneous conversation', since he refused to be recorded talking 'off the cuff (or "Off the Nabocuff," as he said)'.[69] Meanwhile, his writing commitments grew exponentially. In 1964, whilst finalizing the proofs of his *Onegin*, he revised his autobiography, *Conclusive Evidence* (published as *Speak, Memory* in 1967), oversaw the translation and publication of his Russian prose, poetry and drama (most of which was undertaken by Dmitri),[70] and began several new projects – two non-fiction works, *Butterflies of Europe* and *Butterflies in Art*, his Russian *Lolita*, and the essay on time that would begin the evolution of his 1969 novel, *Ada*. At the end of the year he was discussing film ideas with Alfred Hitchcock.[71]

Despite the distractions and interruptions, Nabokov managed to maintain a sense of 'fruitful isolation'[72] and a very civilized daily routine. This combined writing – in his apartment, in the hotel park or by the pool – with excursions into the mountains to hunt butterflies. Every evening, having handed the day's index cards over to Véra 'to be typed and critiqued',[73] he would walk into town to buy his papers from three different stands, in order to be 'democratic with his patronage'.[74] Véra 'provided her analyses over dinner. If she thought something did not work, [Nabokov] explained, he would revise it, and she would retype it'.[75] Véra had always been utterly committed to her husband and was a passionate advocate of everything he did. She provided him with invaluable support in all manner of things in order that nothing interfere with his creative life, and Nabokov adored her. Witness to this was his Bollingen Press editor, Bart Winer: 'When you were in their presence the love flowing from one to another was the most extraordinary thing. I've never seen love like that before.'[76] For Nabokov, the special intimacy of their relationship granted them a unique symbiotic bond:

> I am filled with wonder every time that my random thought or actual sentence is simultaneously voiced by her in those flashes of domestic telepathy whose mystery is only enhanced by their frequency. And I also find enigmatic the stroke of miraculous intuition that makes her find the right words of consolation to give me when something awful, such as a misprint somehow left

Vladimir and Véra, 1966.

uncorrected by me in a recent novel, causes me to plunge into torrents of Russian despair.[77]

In 1965 the peace of Nabokov's world was shattered by Edmund Wilson's attack of his newly published *Eugene Onegin*. Writing in *The New York Review of Books*, Wilson's criticism was directed not simply at the weaknesses of Nabokov's translation and commentary as he perceived them, whereby he questioned Nabokov's techniques and even his understanding of his native language, but also at Nabokov himself. He accused him of having 'bad literary manners', of 'perversity', snobbery and arrogance and even, in a deliberate act of double provocation, described him as having 'sado-masochistic Dostoevskian tendencies', whilst likening his essay on Walter Arndt's recent translation of the poem to 'Marx's niggling and nagging attacks on someone who had the temerity to write about economics and to hold different views'.[78] Wilson had been voicing his objections to Nabokov's anti-Soviet stance and his literary methods since the very beginning of their friendship, objections which Nabokov found baffling. The publication of Pasternak's *Doctor Zhivago* in 1958 strained relations still further – Wilson championed the novel, Nabokov detested it, calling it 'a sorry thing, clumsy, trivial, and melodramatic'.[79] When Nabokov went to Hollywood in 1960 Wilson stopped corresponding altogether – 'You have quite forgotten me', Nabokov wrote, despairingly.[80] Over the next four years, what had been a regular, ebullient exchange became sporadic and perfunctory. In August 1965 Nabokov replied to Wilson's criticism politely but emphatically, suggesting that 'things have gone a little too far'.[81] In March 1971 Nabokov broke nearly six years of silence by writing to Wilson to say that he 'had long ceased to bear [him] a grudge', and had not forgotten 'the warmth of [his] many kindnesses, the various thrills of [their] friendship, that constant excitement of art and intellectual discovery'.[82] Wilson failed to rise to Nabokov's conciliatory gesture, still

Nabokov at one of his favourite newsstands, Montreux.

insisting on the 'ineptitudes' of his *Onegin*, but nevertheless hoping that Nabokov would not take offence at his account of him in a forthcoming book. Despite this, he still attempted, audaciously, to have the last word by accusing Nabokov of mistaking the date in his autobiography of his great-aunt's meeting with Chekhov.[83]

In the last ten years of his life, Nabokov wrote three completely distinct but equally important novels – *Ada*, *Transparent Things* and

Look at the Harlequins! – and began a fourth, *The Original of Laura*, published posthumously in 2009. In *Ada*, dynamics of distortion, corruption and deceit, prevalent in *Lolita* and *Pale Fire*, are magnified to a degree that risks the alienation of all but the most persistent and diligent of readers. The novel's opening premise, 'All happy families are more or less dissimilar; all unhappy ones are more or less alike',[84] deliberately inverts, or everts,[85] the opening statement of Tolstoy's *Anna Karenina* – 'All happy families are alike; every unhappy family is unhappy in its own way'[86] – to instantly establish the guiding principle of Van Veen's chronicle – subversive disorder, disguised as guileless sincerity. As a memoir, *Ada* can be considered in parallel with Nabokov's simultaneously wrought *Speak, Memory*, but also with the autobiographical impulse that dominates *Pale Fire*. Its central theme of incest challenges the last social, sexual and moral taboo, its deviance foreshadowed by the paedophilia of *The Enchanter* and *Lolita*, whilst the affair between brother and sister is presented as romantic love at its most rapturously idyllic and sublimely exalted, unquestioningly deserving of its eventual happy consummation. Meanwhile, the novel extends Nabokov's perennial preoccupation with issues of time, memory, the imagination, creativity and mortality. *Ada*'s 'realism' is distended on multiple planes, from the singular perspective of its trilingual principal narrator, Van Veen, and his manipulation of perspective, chronology, semantics, imagery and literary allusion,[87] to the narrative intrusions of Ada, as well as Violet Knox, Van's secretary, and Roland Oranger, the chronicle's editor, and further still to *Ada*'s antagonistic dual universes, Terra and Antiterra – conflicting realities that are neither autonomous, definitive nor mutually exclusive.

The story is set on Antiterra – an anachronistic amalgam of late nineteenth- and early twentieth-century America, Russia and Europe – and begins in the late 1800s when two supposed cousins, Ada and Van Veen, meet at their family's country estate, Ardis, and fall in love. Van is fourteen and Ada, like Lolita, is twelve, but their passion has an unnervingly adult quality, characterized by extravagant eroticism and unquenchable sexual fervour. Beyond Ardis, circumstance thwarts their attempts to be together, and when discovered by their father, Demon Veen, they are forbidden to see each other. They are finally reunited in late adulthood, long after all those close to them who could possibly be hurt by their relationship are dead.

The purpose of Van's 'ample and delightful chronicle'[88] is, through the deployment of his prodigious memory, to recover the past and immortalize his world in the realm of art. Unlike Nabokov's autobiography, which represents 'the meeting point of an impersonal art form and a very personal life story',[89] Van's memoir is innately unreliable, a 'quicksand of [his] dream-like, dream-rephrased, legend-distorted past'. Van is in his dotage when he embarks upon his project. At 97, he is ill and in pain, is very probably senile and, before he has a chance to approve an 'ideally clean' final draft of his book, dies.[90] The inconsistencies of Van's text can also be considered, however, as an act of 'defiance – Van's intention to record *his* reality, and no other'.[91] Gaps and repetitions, inversions, overlappings, displacements and metamorphoses can thus be read as the deliberately disruptive elements of an ingenious display of intellectual and imaginative pyrotechnics, as devices deployed in an arch demonstration of narrative control and authorial superiority. On the other hand, Van's 'enormous distortions and inaccuracies'[92] also imply the extent to which he has no control. Pivotal to the vitiation of his elaborate construct is another form of disruption, in this instance, unwanted, in the guise of his half-sister, Lucette. One of the 'fond' and the 'frail' she is doomed, 'bound to know anguish and calamity' as a result of her close contact with the progeny of Demon Veen.[93]

If Van and Ada are not already condemned by their selfishness, vulgarity, cruelty and precocious arrogance, then Lucette's tragedy qualifies them as unredeemably despicable. In the same way that Nabokov called Humbert 'horrible', 'abject', and a 'shining example of moral leprosy',[94] he claimed to 'loathe' Van Veen and his 'bitchy and lewd' sister.[95] As he did in *Pale Fire* and *Lolita*, however, Nabokov generates ambivalence by granting his protagonists distinctly positive attributes – the artist's ability to disengage 'from the habit of things', to 'see the web of the world, and the warp and the weft of that web', for example – but like Kinbote and Humbert, Van and Ada's perspective proves to be narrow, reductive and unashamedly mercenary. Ultimately, *Ada* serves as the most potent articulation of Nabokov's claim that,

> far from [being] a frivolous firebird, I was a rigid moralist
> kicking sin, cuffing stupidity, ridiculing the vulgar and
> cruel – and assigning sovereign power to tenderness, talent,
> and pride.[96]

Ada is crucially important in its enactment and elaboration of key Nabokovian preoccupations. For example, he grants his heroine a scientifically acute, super-sensory vision, an eye for detail which delights in combinations that can grant access to higher levels of consciousness – the experience of 'reality' in its most distilled and radiant form. The philosophical system Ada devises to describe these combinations is manifested in sequences of imaginary 'towers' and 'bridges'. A 'tower' is the simultaneous occurrence of three 'things':

> 'real things' which were unfrequent and priceless, simply
> 'things' which formed the routine stuff of life; and 'ghost
> things,' also called 'fogs,' such as fever, toothache, dreadful
> disappointments, and death.[97]

'Bridges' form when three things occur in succession. Ada's 'thing'-oriented perception of reality is, however, countered by Van's scepticism:

'But *this*,' exclaimed Ada, 'is certain, this is reality, this is pure fact – this forest, this moss, your hand, the ladybird on my leg, this cannot be taken away, can it? (it will, it was). *This* has all come together *here*, no matter how the paths twisted, and fooled each other, and got fouled up: they inevitably met here!'[98]

Ada's notion of inevitability is unconvincing to Van, who sees the future 'at every moment' as unpredictable, an 'infinity of branching possibilities'. Yet her argument pre-empts the manner of their eventual coming together at Mont Roux in which a space of 40 years disintegrates under the force of a remembered image and a repeated gesture.[99] The scene enacts the 'thematic designs' whose patterns punctuate Nabokov's autobiography – the spiralling recurrences of Kuropatkin's matches, the shards of pottery on the beach at Mentone, or the butterflies of Utah, the Orodezh and Novaya Zemlya.[100] Van's hypothesis, on the other hand, in which the 'inherent parts of human life' are 'the unknown, the not yet experienced and the unexpected, all the glorious "x" intersections',[101] celebrates a dynamic of indeterminacy which echoes Nabokov's emphasis of 'the isolation, and the strangeness, of so-called reality'. This, he argued, is a perspective that 'constantly characterizes the artist, the genius, the discoverer', whereas Ada's confidence in her ability to grasp the 'real' aligns her with those 'mediocrities' who base their sense of reality on an expectation of 'continuity' or 'duration'.[102] Nabokov's assignment of different aspects of his personal and artistic philosophies to *Ada*'s protagonists both dramatizes and creates a new context in which to explore their contradictions and complexities. Meanwhile, the persistent vacillation between opposing standpoints generates a tension that is never fully resolved, and presents Nabokov's most direct and provocative challenge to his readers.

The essay that Van composes on his journey to Mont Roux – 'The Texture of Time' – is concerned less with the problem of reality than it is with the degenerative force of time that consigns 'the glittering "now"' to the 'colored nothingness' of the past and leads, inexorably, to future's 'absolute nothing'.[103] Informed by Proust's handling of time and memory and the theories of Bergson and Whitrow,[104] Van's attempt to define the 'essence of Time' is driven by a fundamental Nabokovian impulse – to make the intangible tangible, to 'indulge in a simulacrum of possession'.[105] He sets out to solve what Adam Krug describes as the 'inner' problem of 'life, thought, love, the unknown within', and 'their point of contact (death)', but has no interest in the larger 'outer' problem of 'space, time, matter, the unknown without'.[106] His enquiry is focused on the physiological and philosophical experience of lived time as a 'sense of continuous becoming', of 'memory in the making'. Like Nabokov, he does not believe in the conventional concept of three-dimensional time. Nabokov's contention that 'the present is only the top of the past, and the future does not exist',[107] is echoed by Van's argument that 'there are only two panels. The Past (ever-existing in my mind) and the Present (to which my mind gives duration and, therefore, reality)'.[108] Nevertheless, Van's 'perception of the conjunction of past and present, rather than giving him a sense of liberation from time, makes him even more acutely aware of its immediate impingement'.[109] Time may impinge, but it is not related to, say, the dilemma of mortality, which Nabokov experienced as 'the utter degradation, ridicule, and horror of having developed an infinity of sensation and thought within a finite existence'. Van's perspective rejects the negative prospect of an 'impersonal darkness', of infinity's 'inadmissible abyss'. Rather, it triumphantly enacts (whilst oblivious to the irony), Krug's delineation of a vision 'adulterated by the concept of "time"':

> certain mind pictures have become so adulterated by the concept of 'time' that we have come to believe in the actual existence of a permanently moving bright fissure (the point

of perception) between our retrospective eternity which we cannot recall and the prospective one which we cannot know.[110]

Van is precisely that 'permanently moving bright fissure'.

Whilst Van may be 'able to delight sensually in the texture of time, "in its stuff and spread, in the fall of its folds, in the very impalpability of its grayish gauze, in the coolness of its continuum"', ultimately, over and above his identification of time 'as the dim hollow between two rhythmic beats',[111] his investigation fails. Ada's response – 'We can know the time, we can know a time. We can never know Time. Our senses are simply not meant to perceive it'[112] – not only dismisses Van's enquiry as futile, but also echoes Nabokov's own emphatic stance – 'Electricity. Time. Space. We know *nothing* about these things.'[113]

In Nabokov's world, the 'robust reality' of a remembered past has the power to make 'a ghost of the present', such that 'nothing will ever change' and 'nobody will ever die'.[114] In Van's malleable universe, like the folds of Nabokov's magic carpet, the past manifests itself as 'a constant accumulation of images [that] can be easily contemplated and listened to, tested and tasted at random, so that it ceases to mean the orderly alternation of linked events that it does in the large theoretical sense'.[115] Whilst Van may prove a failed philosopher, as an artist he succeeds in producing a text which answers his debate on space and time. Van's chronicle, by 'transvers[ing] inconvenient space and collaps[ing] oppressive time',[116] realizes his dream of 'a "primitive" form of Time', in which 'the Past [is] not yet clearly differentiated from the Present, so that past shadows and shapes [show] through the still soft, long, larval "now"'.[117]

The guiding principle of Van's memoir is to assume control over chaos. 'In "real" life', he says, 'we are creatures of chance in an absolute world – unless we are artists ourselves'.[118] His artistic endeavour is essentially a corruption of Nabokov's mnemonic process of 'artistic selection, artistic blending, artistic re-combination',[119] and his reconfiguration of the past produces a lie as unscrupulous as the edited version of her life that Ada's mother, the film actress Marina Durmanov, envisages:

> Someday, she mused, one's past must be put in order. Retouched, retaken. Certain 'wipes' and 'inserts' will have to be made in the picture; certain telltale abrasions in the emulsion will have to be corrected; 'dissolves' in the sequence discreetly combined with the trimming out of the unwanted, embarrassing 'footage' and definite guarantees obtained; yes, someday – before death with its clapstick closes the scene.[120]

The extent to which Van 're-touches' his past qualifies him as a 'bad memoirist'. From Nabokov's perspective, such activity results in 'a blue-tinted or pink-shaded photograph taken by a stranger to console sentimental bereavement'.[121] Beneath its dazzling surface, Van's devious chronicle produces something far darker than the blue tints and pink shades of a retouched photograph, but it serves a similar purpose – to console his sentimental nostalgia for a lost Eden, and his regret for his part in the destruction of an innocent life.

7

The Final Arc, 1969–77

We live surrounded by more or less ghostly objects.[1]

Decades before, V. D. Nabokov had given his son a copy of Flaubert's *Madame Bovary*, with the inscription 'livre génial – la perle de la littérature française'. Now, on the flyleaf of his own personal copy of *Ada* Nabokov wrote, 'a book of genius – the pearl of American literature'.[2] Nabokov's claim to be an American writer was founded on a variety of things – on his citizenship, on the fact that he had spent nearly twenty years there, that it had provided the settings and the inspiration for his most celebrated work. In terms of the place of his fiction in the American literary tradition, it is not insignificant that his 'American period coincided almost exactly with the rise of postmodernism'.[3] The first major postmodernist novel, William Gaddis's *The Recognitions*, was published in 1955, the same year as *Lolita*, and although Nabokov was to know 'little or nothing about' the postmodernists, 'they knew much about him and often were afraid of being eclipsed by him'.[4] Meanwhile, at Cornell, Nabokov influenced a whole generation of American writers – including Thomas Pynchon, who was a member of a Nabokov cult – with his controversial, anti-realist stance – 'Nothing ages faster than "stark realism"', he would advise his students.[5]

The four key characteristics of the postmodernist text have been defined as 'war with the audience, self-consciousness, the dream of an ahistorical literature, and disinterest in communicating meanings'.[6] To this can be added concerns with the hyper-real and multiple worlds, simulation, inauthenticity, absence, elision, erasure, exhibitionism and resistance. *Ada* demonstrates every one of these concerns but they can equally be identified as prevailing aspects of Nabokov's art that extend to his very last novel, *The Original of Laura*. Similarly, *Pale Fire* could be described as a 'text-oriented' novel with 'no pre-textual reality', a postmodern imperative that can also be traced back to his earliest fiction.

Nabokov stubbornly resisted any form of categorization, yet his contentious emphasis on 'the inherent morality of uninhibited art',[7] on writing as a form of mystification – 'a great writer is always a great enchanter'[8] – on style – 'I am almost exclusively a writer, and my style is all I have'[9] – echoes the antagonistic, anti-rational, anti-conventional postmodernist stance and its constructionist treatment of the mechanics of art. The notion, voiced by Adam Krug, that 'we speak of one thing being like some other thing when what we are really craving to do is to describe something that is like nothing on earth',[10] anticipates the postmodernist dynamic of epistemological uncertainty, but also expresses Nabokov's abiding preoccupation with and investigation into other worlds and other states of being across his English and Russian fiction which defies limiting alignment with any specific literary movement. Ultimately, the 'main favor' he asked of any 'serious critic' was that they have

> sufficient perceptiveness to understand that whatever term or trope I use, my purpose is not to be facetiously flashy or grotesquely obscure but to express what I feel and think with the utmost truthfulness and perception.[11]

With the publication of *Ada*, Nabokov made the cover of *Time* magazine, but his audience was also beginning to extend beyond Western Europe. Although the Soviets considered him an ideological enemy and refused to publish his work, copies of his early novels were clandestinely circulated. Underground interest was encouraged by the publication of his Russian *Lolita* in 1967 and the reprinting of his early fiction by a Michigan-based publisher, Ardis, which began soon after. Since Nabokov's rehabilitation in the mid-1980s, when he was dubbed '*the* writer of perestroika',[12] authoritative editions of his entire Russian catalogue have appeared. His St Petersburg home is now a museum and the Rozhdestveno estate a designated tourist site.

In the last decade of his life, Nabokov focused on the global dissemination of his work. Along with the translation of his Russian stories, poems, plays and novels, one of his most demanding projects was the French version of *Ada*, which appeared in 1975. Although he had already abandoned his *Butterflies of Europe*, he continued to research *Butterflies in Art*, and on summer vacations combined butterfly hunting in Portugal, Sicily and the South of France, the Swiss Alps or the Pyrenees with trips to Italian art galleries.

Apart from the achievement of *Ada* and the release of Tony Richardson's film version of *Laughter in the Dark*, one of the highlights of 1969 was the Apollo moon landing, which Nabokov watched on a specially rented TV. Imagining the astronauts' experience to be 'the most remarkable romantic thrill ever experienced in the history of discovery' he was enraptured by the thought of

the absolutely overwhelming excitement of the adventure, the strange sensual exhilaration of palpating those precious pebbles, of seeing our marbled globe in the black sky, of feeling along one's spine the shiver and wonder of it.[13]

Over the next year Nabokov wrote a sixteenth novel, finalized revised translations of *Mary*, *Glory* and *Eugene Onegin*, and compiled a volume of poems and chess problems. In the summer of 1970 he met with Alan Jay Lerner, who wanted to produce a musical of *Lolita*. Although Nabokov was enthusiastic, the show's opening weeks were a critical disaster and *Lolita, My Love* closed before it

In Montreux, 1968.

reached Broadway. In 1971 the British director Donald Cammell sent Nabokov his 'Notes on a Film of PALE FIRE'. Nabokov was 'absolutely delighted' with them and wrote back to Cammell, describing his ideas as 'fascinating' and 'beautifully presented',[14] but the film was never made. *King, Queen, Knave*, however, directed by Jerzy Skoli-mowski and starring David Niven and Gina Lollobrigida, was nominated for the Palme d'Or at Cannes in May 1972. Just a month before, Nabokov had completed his short but intricately wrought *Transparent Things*.

After the decadent opulence of *Ada*, *Transparent Things* initially seems obtusely slight and inconsequential. Unlike the sophisticated and manipulative Van Veen, Nabokov's hero, Hugh Person, is a 'sentimental simpleton',[15] a misfit, a man persistently out of his depth, afflicted by irrational fears and compromised at every turn.

Set alternately in New York and Witt, a small ski resort in the Swiss Alps, it recounts four trips Hugh makes to Switzerland over eighteen years. On the first, aged 22, he accompanies his father, recently widowed, who collapses and dies in a shop whilst trying on a pair of trousers. Ten years later Hugh returns, this time in the role of editor, for a meeting with the celebrated novelist, R. It is on this trip that he meets and marries the eccentric and coldly promiscuous Armande Chamar. Back in New York, after a third trip, Hugh, a victim of nightmares and somnambulism since child-hood, strangles Armande in his sleep, believing, in a dream, that he is rescuing her from the window of a burning building. Convicted of murder he is incarcerated and subjected, unsuccessfully, to psychoanalysis. On his release, Hugh, now 40, makes his last trip to Witt in an attempt to relive the few happy weeks spent with Armande. Intent on returning to the same hotel where he stayed eight years before, he hopes, like Chorb, to somehow initiate 'a moment of contact' with his dead wife's 'essential image'.[16] His mission, how-ever, is a failure, and he dies in a fire at the wrong hotel.

Transparent Things is the first major work since Nabokov's early Russian stories – 'Natasha' and 'A Busy Man', for example – to delineate a palpable spirit world. In *The Real Life of Sebastian Knight*, Sebastian's presence is suggested but never made fully explicit. Similarly, the world of the Vane sisters remains veiled until the reader unravels their acrostic at the end of the story, and in *Pale Fire* and *Ada*, ghostly interference is either barely perceptible or frustratingly obtuse.[17] Here, however, Hugh's world is peopled by 'umbral companions'.[18] His story is narrated by the ghost of the writer R., beginning and ending with Hugh being greeted by a host of spirits as he makes his transition into the afterlife. From his privileged perspective and in a series of time-defying flashbacks, R. recounts Hugh's life with laconic detachment, all the while remaining sympathetic to his anguish and frustration – a 'tender ghost humoring a lucky mortal'.[19] R.'s perspective grants the reader an insight into the patterning of motifs that determine Hugh's fate, yet R. has no power to intervene or change its inevitable course. Ironically, whilst these lethal motifs, which take the form of a kind of diabolic trinity – fire, asphyxiation and falling – abound, and are the focus of Hugh's phobias, his ineptitude renders him incapable of either apprehending their pattern or interpreting their significance.

Like Chorb and Luzhin, Hugh is 'harrowed by coincident symbols', but R.'s perspective proves his fears to be unfounded. The flames that mean a violent, painful death to Hugh are, in R.'s world, benign, even protective. In the most explicit depiction of the otherworld anywhere in Nabokov's fiction, they subtly assist Hugh's transition into the afterlife by guiding him away from the burning window to which he is instinctively drawn. Likewise, Hugh's fear of falling is to R. a mere inconvenience. His focus is not on the potential deadly crush of gravity but, rather, on the business of negotiating his world in order to 'remain in the now'. 'A thin veneer of immediate reality is spread over natural and artificial matter', he argues, 'and whoever wishes to remain in the now, with the now, on the now, should please not break its tension film'.[20] R. experiences time and space as levels that drop away into infinity, which emulates Nabokov's notion of reality as 'an infinite succession of steps, levels of perception, false bottoms'. Reminiscent of John Shade's 'glissading' ghosts,[21] R. can, if he chooses, exist in the entire history of a place all at once, each level of time, as it were, overlapping and coinciding in a kind of metaphysical 'cosmic synchronisation'. Meanwhile, the barriers of Hugh's world form the tangible boundaries of his existence, setting the limitations of his consciousness and magnifying the intensity of his solitude. Like Ivanov in 'Perfection', whose consciousness 'flutters and walks up and down the glass pane which for as long as he lived would prevent him from having direct contact with the world',[22] Hugh is acutely aware of the barriers that constrain him, from the sky's 'meniscus' and the glass walls that confront him at every angle, to his own 'dazzled and watery eyes'. Hugh perceives such surfaces as impenetrable obstructions, which at the same time enclose and protect him from the yawning abysses that lie behind them, but for R. they provide a means of halting an infinite perceptual fall, and simply define layers of time and space. Hugh's barriers are vertical and grounded by gravity, whereas R.'s float horizontally in an endless series of transparent layers. Only in a dream does Hugh experience R.'s point of view, as he visualizes the layers of cloud which 'seem to lie on a flat sheet of glass in a celestial laboratory'[23] from the window of an aeroplane at 30,000 feet. In this gravity-defying dream-state, Hugh is granted a momentary vision of R.'s world, and it is a world free of fear.

Transparent Things offers the most conclusive resolution of Nabokov's abiding preoccupation with the boundaries of mortality. Throughout his fiction, Nabokov's protagonists are tantalized by the elusive presence of the hereafter which seems to stand 'slightly ajar in the dark'.[24] In *Lolita*, Humbert suggests that the afterlife may be nothing more than 'an eternal state of excruciating insanity'.[25] Pnin, on the other hand, envisages it as 'a kind of soundlessly spinning ethereal void',[26] similar to the infinite blackness of John Shade's 'spiral types of space'.[27] Krug's question, that 'death is either the instantaneous gaining of perfect knowledge' or 'absolute nothingness' is finally answered here. Hugh's transformation into a fluid, transparent entity enacts Nabokov's concept of death as a 'divestment' or 'communion'. This is '*it*', says R., 'not the crude anguish of physical death but the incomparable pangs of the mysterious mental maneuver needed to pass from one state of being to another'.[28] In death, Hugh, like R. and his 'umbral companions', achieves the 'infinite consciousness', or 'supersensory insight into the world' that the philosopher Pierre Delalande predicts in *The Gift*. With 'the disintegration of the body', Delalande posits, the soul is liberated 'from the eye-sockets of the flesh' and, in a curious echo of Smurov's ideal, incorporeal state, transformed 'into one complete and free eye, which can simultaneously see in all directions'.[29] Man may only exist 'insofar as he is separated from his surroundings', but the divestment, in death, of the 'film of flesh' that 'envelops' him[30] does not necessarily initiate the disintegration of his spirit. 'Human life,' Nabokov argued, 'is but a first instalment of the serial soul', and 'one's individual secret is not lost in the process of earthly dissolution'.[31] Whilst for Lucette, and also probably Hazel, death amounts to 'only a more complete assortment of the infinite fractions of solitude', for Nabokov it promises release into a much-desired 'free world of timelessness'.[32]

Although *Transparent Things* may provide the 'simple solution to the universe' that so eludes Pnin,[33] it also reasserts the problem of identifying, defining and capturing reality that is the main preoccupation of Nabokov's next novel, *Look at the Harlequins!* 'Men have learned to live with a black burden', says R.,

> a huge aching lump: the supposition that 'reality' may only be a 'dream.' How much more dreadful it would be if the very awareness of your being aware of reality's dreamlike nature were also a dream, a built-in hallucination![34]

Nabokov's last complete novel was finished on 3 April 1974, just three weeks before his 75th birthday. He had been particularly

Nabokov with butterfly book, 1965.

nervous whilst working on it, developing a morbid fear that he would die, leaving it unfinished. In an unprecedented move, he numbered all the index cards that comprised final drafts, stipulating that only the numbered cards could be preserved for publication in the event of his death. The novel's completion gave Nabokov a new lease of life – he immediately signed a new four-year, six-book contract with McGraw-Hill, which would include a new work, *The Original of Laura*.

Nabokov's anxiety was exacerbated by the problems he was experiencing with his biographer, Andrew Field. Nabokov had agreed to the project in 1968, but realized, when Field presented his first draft five years later, that he had made a dreadful mistake. Nabokov was appalled by the 'number of absurd errors, impossible statements, vulgarities and inventions' in Field's draft,[35] but his serial attempts to correct its inaccuracies and misinterpretations drew him into a protracted and increasingly acrimonious conflict which he eventually abandoned to his lawyers. When Field's 'nauseatingly mannered and self-important' 'vast compendium of error' was finally published in 1977 as *Vladimir Nabokov: His Life in Part*, Nabokov was too ill to look at it.[36]

Look at the Harlequins! was very much devised in response to the 'rot and nastiness' of Field's work,[37] but also belongs, in its self-consciousness and self-referentiality, its darkly comic exhibitionism and fraudulence, with the paranoid, duplicitous narratives of *Pale Fire* and *Ada*.[38] A retrospective of the life and loves of a Russian émigré author, Vadim Vadimovich, its details reverberate disarmingly with elements of Nabokov's own autobiography. Like Nabokov, Vadim is born into an aristocratic Russian family at the turn of the twentieth century and forced into exile in Europe and the United States. Unlike Nabokov, Vadim is plagued by bouts of insanity and a series of disastrous romantic entanglements. He marries four times, eventually finding his 'defense against cosmic horror' in his equivalent to Nabokov's Véra, the anonymous You, at the very end of his life.

Vadim's literary career closely parallels Nabokov's – its chronology and location, its transition from Russian to English. The titles and content of his work share striking similarities to an extent where, much to his annoyance, Vadim is frequently mistaken for another writer. Nagged by the suspicion that he is in fact 'the non-identical twin, a parody, a variant of another man's life, somewhere on this or another earth', he senses that some 'demon' is forcing him to 'impersonate that other man' who 'was and would always be incomparably greater, healthier, and crueler than your obedient servant'.[39] This figure can be identified either as Vadim's alter ego, the 'sane' half of his consciousness which intermittently infiltrates Vadim's 'fanciful' universe or Vladimir Nabokov. Apart from his fiction, Vadim shares many of Nabokov's distinctive qualities, whilst both his abandoned pen-name, V. Irisin, and the name of his first wife Iris, are an anagram and partial palindrome of Sirin. If the stranger is Nabokov, then, for the first time since his 'visits of inspection' in *King, Queen Knave* or the interventions of *Bend Sinister*, he has ceased to be a merely involute presence and has begun to emerge into the world of his novel, even if only in an indistinct, partial form.[40] This figure, 'N', who is also oddly reminiscent of *Pnin*'s elusive N—, whilst seeming to intrude from another, parallel universe, is also an aspect of Vadim's hermetic system, and thus possibly simply another element of what is, essentially, an elaborate, delusive, self-referential construct.

Vadim is already 'harbouring the secrets of a confirmed madman' at the age of seven or eight when his grand aunt implores him to 'Look at the harlequins!' Through the course of his life he suffers several catastrophic mental and physical breakdowns, triggered by temporal-spatial panic. Unlike Hugh's vertigo, which is, more conventionally, altitudinal, Vadim's is pivotal, provoked by the mere thought of making a 180-degree turn and retracing his steps, a prospect he perceives as akin to reversing time. This, combined with a faulty memory, a propensity to drink too much and a tendency for paranoid scepticism, profoundly undermines his reliability as a narrator. He frequently defers to a sabotaging force reminiscent of Humbert's McFate which he perceives as a 'clumsy conspiracy [by] a main plotter' who 'insisted on making inept moves that seemed to preclude the slightest possibility of success'.[41] At the same time, Nabokov's notion of metaphysical design, of 'secret themes concealed within a visible destiny',[42] is presented in recurring patterns of distinct motifs – harlequins, angels, butterflies, flowers and rainbows – that prove ultimately to be nothing more than the empty projections of a crazed mind.

During the delirium of his final seizure Vadim searches for his real name, haunted by the shadow of the anonymous 'N'. Further corroding his sense of self, Vadim assumes the characteristics of many of his (or more recognizably, Nabokov's) fictional protagonists. In his preoccupation with the presence of a double he resembles Smurov or Hermann Karlovich. His escape from revolutionary

Russia reads like Kinbote's from Zembla. His relationship with Bel is unsettlingly similar to Humbert's with Lolita, and his solipsistic retrospective stance is highly reminiscent of Van Veen's narcissistic egotism. The duality that infects every aspect of Vadim's world reflects the dual nature of the Nabokovian artist, whose 'necessary two-sidedness' enables him to 'live in one world while he creates another'. Critically, however, Vadim fails 'to recognize the treacherousness of the created world of words'.[43] The eventual assertion of what Vadim claims to be 'reality' comes with the arrival of You, her entrance marked, appropriately, by a triple harlequin (reminiscent of one of Ada's towers), and it is the 'reality of her radiance'[44] that finally causes Vadim's solipsistic universe to dissolve.

Across his fiction, Nabokov asserts that 'love and artistic creation are the only transcendent realities', but they are also 'personal mysteries, impenetrable to outsiders'.[45] If the novel is read as Nabokov's 'oblique tribute to his first meeting with Véra', then its very title and harlequin theme, along with its opening chapters, which establish the premise of Vadim's memoir and the manner in which he meets his first wife, Iris, underpins and ultimately sanctions what at first seems an incongruous, unconvincing dénouement. Nabokov's private title for the book was, after all, *Look at the Masks!*[46]

By May 1974 Nabokov had what would have been his eighteenth novel 'mapped out rather clearly for next year'. *The Original of Laura* he saw as 'Inspiration. Radiant insomnia. The flavour of snow of beloved alpine slopes. A novel *without* an I, without a he, but with the narrator, *the gliding eye*, being implied throughout'.[47] He spent the summer butterfly hunting in the Swiss Alps and northern Italy and, for the rest of the year and into the following spring, was absorbed with final revisions of his French *Ada* and the translation of a last set of Russian stories. In July 1975 he was back on his beloved alpine slopes chasing butterflies but fell badly and lay helpless for over two hours before being rescued. In December, following an operation on a benign prostate tumour, he returned 'zestfully to the abyss' of his new novel, and by April 1976 was pleased to report that he was 'proceeding at the rate of 5 or 6 cards per day, but a lot of rewriting'. He had 'transcribed in final form 50 cards = 5000 words', and by end of the month had completed over 100 pages, planning to finish by the autumn. His schedule was disrupted again, however, by another fall a few weeks later. Greatly weakened, he was hospitalized from July to September with a debilitating infection. In his delirium he would see himself in a 'walled garden', reading his new novel to 'a small dream audience' of 'peacocks, pigeons, my long-dead parents, two cypresses, several young nurses crouching around, and a family doctor so old as to be

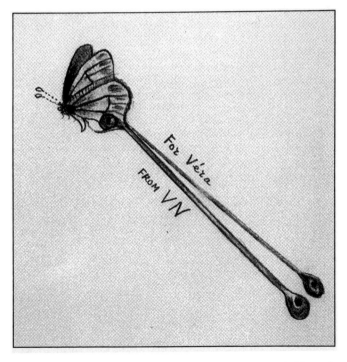

One of Nabokov's many fantastical butterfly illustrations. He dedicated all his work to Véra.

almost invisible'.[48] Over the winter he seemed unable to regain his strength and in March 1977 developed a fever that turned into a severe bronchial infection from which he died on 2 July. A few days before, Dmitri had noticed tears welling up in his father's eyes. When he asked what was wrong, Nabokov replied 'that a certain butterfly was already on the wing; and his eyes told me that he no longer hoped that he would live to pursue it again'.[49]

Nabokov's last work lay in a Swiss bank vault for over 30 years before finally being published in November 2009. He had left express instructions that it be burnt if he was unable to complete it, ever wary of allowing anything but an absolute final version to be seen. 'Only ambitious nonentities and hearty mediocrities exhibit their rough drafts', he once argued. 'It is like passing around samples of one's sputum.'[50] Neither Véra nor Dmitri could bring themselves to destroy the manuscript, however, and in 2008 Dmitri decided that there was enough in the extant 138 index cards to provide a clear sense of his father's plan for *The Original of Laura: Dying is Fun*. A discernable narrative sequence is contained in just over 60 numbered cards with the remainder comprising a distinct series of sections and scenes alongside fragmentary notes, sketches and thoughts. Together they offer a tantalizing but equally frustrating glimpse of a work that promised to be one of Nabokov's most elaborately conceived and innovative designs.

With the translucent quality of *Transparent Things* and a technical complexity that recalls *The Gift*, *The Original of Laura* investigates truth and its source – originality – notions which prove as elusive as Nabokov's concept of an 'unquenchable, unattainable' reality. The novel's title refers to *My Laura* or *Laura*, a scurrilous semi-autobiographical novel written by a former lover of Laura's 'original', Flora Wild. A 'maddening masterpiece', its heroine is shamelessly unfaithful, coldly acquisitive and subjected to the 'craziest death in the world'.[51]

Flora is American born to Russian émigrés – a promiscuous ballerina and a bisexual photographer. Her father commits suicide,

shooting himself simultaneously with a camera and a gun, and
she grows up in a household of many 'uncles', one of whom,
'prowling' and 'pushing', serially molests her. In her early twenties
she marries Philip Wild, a lecturer in experimental psychology
and 'an authority on dreams'. 'Fat', 'fierce' and 40 years her senior,
he compulsively undertakes a series of bizarre experiments which
he is writing up in the form of 'a mad neurologist's testament'. By
picturing himself as an erasable, vertical white line on the plum-
coloured inside walls of his closed eyelids, Wild 'woos' death by
indulging in a 'perilous' but reversible process of 'auto-dissolution'
which, he claims, affords 'the greatest ecstasy known to man'.[52]

My Laura haunts the narrative, at points converging with and
even displacing it, whilst the identities of *Laura*'s 'I' and the author
of Flora's story remain teasingly obscure. Meanwhile, the novel's
already compromised theme of originality is further mitigated by
other books within the book – Wild's 'testament' which is also a
memoir of sorts, a 'Medical Intermezzo' featuring A.N.D., and
'Eric's notes'. Each have their own autonomous quality yet are
bewilderingly interconnected by obliquely recurring motifs and
allusions that signal the operation of the novel's ubiquitous *gliding
eye*, guided, of course, by Nabokov. Ultimately, however, *The Original
of Laura* is as fragile as the 'marvellous soap bubble' imagined
by Smurov almost 50 years before. Just as it begins to 'grow' and
'expand' it 'suddenly is no longer there, and all that remains is
a snitch of ticklish moisture that hits you in the face'.[53]

Nabokov saw himself as one of many Russians of his generation
who had 'passed through a period of genius, as if destiny were loyally
trying what it could for them by giving them more than their share,
in view of the cataclysm that was to remove completely the world
they had known'.[54] He never wanted to go back to Russia, knowing
that it could be nothing like the country he remembered. 'The Russia
I need is always with me,' he insisted, 'literature, language, and my
own Russian childhood.'[55] The landscape of America had offered

Butterfly hunting, Switzerland.

him the closest approximation to the woods and marshes of Vyra, and he was then able to replicate his favourite butterfly-hunting grounds in the mountains of Switzerland. Nevertheless, he always hoped to return to America, where his 'ideal arrangement would be an absolutely soundproofed flat in New York, on a top floor', and 'a bungalow in the Southwest'. His American experience had, after all, transformed his life. When asked how he saw himself in the world of letters, Nabokov replied, 'Jolly good view from up here', but he remained modest about his success – '*Lolita* is famous, not I. I am an obscure, doubly obscure, novelist with an unpronounceable name.'[56] Yet his sense of himself, his life and his art is perhaps best expressed by the answer he gave to a reporter on his 72nd birthday. 'Asked what his wishes for himself would be, if wishes were horses', he replied, 'in the clearest of phrases: "Pegasus, only Pegasus."'[57]

References

1 'Nothing will ever change, nobody will ever die'

1 Vladimir Nabokov, *Speak, Memory: An Autobiography Revisited* (New York, 1999), p. 56.
2 The date shifted to 23 April, coincidentally, Shakespeare's birthday, when calendars adjusted at the turn of the twentieth century. See ibid., pp. 6–7.
3 Ibid., p. 25.
4 Nabokov describes being drawn to the butterfly by his 'guiding angel (whose wings, except for the absence of a Florentine limbus, resemble those of Fra Angelico's Gabriel)'. Ibid., p. 90.
5 Ibid., pp. 91, 93.
6 See ibid., pp. 23–5.
7 Andrew Field, *Nabokov: His Life in Part* (London, 1977), p. 87.
8 *Speak, Memory*, p. 22.
9 Vladimir Nabokov, *Strong Opinions* (New York, 1973), p. 81.
10 For more detail, see Don Barton Johnson, 'Nabokov's Golliwoggs: Lodi Reads English 1899–1909', *Zembla*, at www.libraries.psu.edu/nabokov/dbjg04.htm.
11 Letter to Edmund Wilson, 5 May 1950, in *Dear Bunny, Dear Volodya: The Nabokov-Wilson Letters, 1940–1971*, ed. S. Karlinsky (Berkeley and Los Angeles, CA, 2001), p. 268.
12 Brian Boyd, *Vladimir Nabokov: The Russian Years* (London, 1993), p. 91.
13 Nabokov's life-long admiration of Wells was initiated by Wells's visit to 47 Bol´shaya Morskaya in 1914. See ibid., p. 178n.
14 Karlinsky, ed., *Nabokov-Wilson Letters*, p. 246.

15 Joseph Hessen, cited in Field, *His Life in Part*, p. 92.

16 Boyd, *The Russian Years*, p. 105.

17 *Speak, Memory*, p. 134.

18 See Brian Boyd, 'New Light on Nabokov's Russian Years', *Cycnos*, x/1 (1993), at http://revel.unice.fr/cycnos/document.html?id=1281.

19 *Speak, Memory*, p. 71.

20 Ibid., p. 135.

21 Ibid., p. 114.

22 Founded in the late 1890s, over five years it published a magazine with Sergey Diaghilev as its chief editor. It later supported contemporary artists, including Mikhail Nesterov, Mikhail Vrubel and Isaac Levitan, by sponsoring exhibitions of their work. Many of its members contributed to the staging and design of productions for Stanislavsky's Moscow Art Theatre and Diaghilev's Ballets Russes.

23 *Speak, Memory*, p. 179.

24 Ibid., p. 169.

25 Boyd, *The Russian Years*, p. 118.

26 *Speak, Memory*, p. 185.

27 Boyd, *The Russian Years*, p. 121.

28 *Speak, Memory*, p. 187.

29 Boyd, *The Russian Years*, p. 132.

30 Excerpt from 'Petrograd 25 October [7 November] 1917', published in Gennady Barabtarlo, 'Nabokov's Reliquary Poem', *The Russian Review*, LII/4 (October 1993), pp. 540–46 (p. 545), and *Aerial View: Essays on Nabokov's Art and Metaphysics* (New York, 1993), p. 253.

31 *Speak, Memory*, p. 189.

32 Boyd, *The Russian Years*, p. 140.

33 Ibid., p. 141.

34 Most of Nabokov's early unpublished poems were lost. These three appeared at the time in local newspapers. The earliest of his poems in print is 'The Rain has Flown' (1917), which opens his 1971 selection of Russian and English verse, *Poems and Problems* (New York, 1970).

35 Boyd, *The Russian Years*, p. 150.

36 *Speak, Memory*, pp. 196, 191.

37 Andrew Field, *Nabokov: His Life in Art* (London, 1967), p. 63.

38 Vladimir Nabokoff, 'Remembrance', *The English Review*, 144 (November 1920), p. 392.

39 Vladimir Nabokov, *The Collected Stories* (London, 2001), p. 5.

40 See his comment in a 1970 interview: *Strong Opinions*, p. 161. See also, 'On Nabokov's Pen Name Sirin', in Gavriel Shapiro, *Delicate Markers: Subtexts in Vladimir Nabokov's 'Invitation to a Beheading'* (New York, 1998), pp. 9–29.

41 For more, see Michael Kellogg, 'Hitler's "Russian" Connection: White Émigré Influence on the Genesis of Nazi Ideology, 1917–1923', at www.sscnet.ucla.edu/soc/groups/scr/kellogg.pdf.

42 Boyd, *The Russian Years*, pp. 193–4.

43 Ibid., p. 196.

44 Stacy Schiff, *Véra (Mrs Vladimir Nabokov): Portrait of a Marriage* (New York, 1999), p. 6.

45 Boyd, *The Russian Years*, p. 206.

46 Schiff, *Véra*, p. 6.

47 Boyd, *The Russian Years*, pp. 207–8.

48 Matthew J. Bruccoli and Dmitri Nabokov, eds, *Vladimir Nabokov: Selected Letters, 1940–77* (London, 1991), p. 59.

49 Vladimir Nabokov, *Mary* (London, 1973), p. 10.

50 Boyd, *The Russian Years*, p. 257.

51 Vladimir E. Alexandrov, ed., *The Garland Companion to Vladimir Nabokov* (New York, 1995), pp. 356, 355.

52 *Mary*, p. 9.

53 Ibid., p. 7.

54 *Speak, Memory*, p. 56. Ganin's mnemonic recall has a distinctly Proustian quality, but there is no evidence that Nabokov fully engaged with Proust's work until the mid-1930s. See *Strong Opinions*, p. 57 and John Burt Foster, Jr, *Nabokov's Art of Memory and European Modernism* (Princeton, NJ, 1993).

55 *Mary*, p. 40.

56 Vladimir Nabokov, *King, Queen, Knave* (London, 1993), pp. v–vi.

57 Published for the first time in English by Dmitri Nabokov in *The New Yorker* (26 December 2005), at www.newyorker.com/archive/2005/12/26/051226fi_fiction2.

58 *Collected Stories*, pp. 140, 78.

59 The play has only recently been published. See Vladimir Nabokov, *'Tragediia gospodina Morna'; Pesy; Lektsii o drame* (St Petersburg, 2008). For commentary, see Boyd, *The Russian Years*, pp. 222–6.

60 Vladimir Nabokov, 'The Art of Literature and Commonsense', in *Lectures on Literature* (San Diego, CA, 1980), p. 374.

61 *Collected Stories*, pp. 49, 50.

62 Ibid., p. 145.

63 Ibid., p. 146.

64 Michael Glynn, *Vladimir Nabokov: Bergsonian and Russian Formalist Influences in His Novels* (Basingstoke, 2007), p. 75. 'Nabokov was a Bergson enthusiast. He had been intensely stimulated by Bergson's philosophy, especially during his European émigré phase' (p. 53). See also *Strong Opinions*, p. 43.

65 It is likely that Nabokov directly encountered the work of the Russian Formalist Viktor Shklovsky, who was in Berlin from 1922–3, where he published 'a number of journal articles, his quirky epistolary novel, *Zoo, or Letters Not about Love*; a volume of autobiography, *A Sentimental Journey* and a collection of essays, *Knight's Move*'. Glynn, *Vladimir Nabokov*, p. 35.

66 Steven Cassedy, ed., *Selected Essays of Andrey Bely* (Stanford, CA, 1995), p. 69.

67 *Collected Stories*, p. 180.

2 Sirin, Part One: 'Terror' to *The Eye*

1 Vladimir Nabokov, *Strong Opinions* (New York, 1973), pp. 154–5. Also Vladimir Nabokov, *Mary* (London, 1973), p. 10.

2 Vladimir E. Alexandrov, ed., *The Garland Companion to Vladimir Nabokov* (New York, 1995), pp. 349–50.

3 'He later recalled that he never once paid for a book in Berlin, but read whole tomes little by little in the bookshops.' Brian Boyd, *Vladimir Nabokov: The Russian Years* (London, 1993), p. 263.

4 Ibid., pp. 259, 244.

5 Vladimir Nabokov, *The Collected Stories* (London, 2001), p. 648.

6 Stacy Schiff, *Véra (Mrs Vladimir Nabokov): Portrait of a Marriage* (New York, 1999), p. 67.

7 Vladimir Nabokov, *King, Queen, Knave* (London, 1993), p. v.

8 Herbert Gold, 'Nabokov Remembered: A Slight Case of Poshlost', in *The Achievements of Vladimir Nabokov: Essays, Studies, Reminiscences*

   and Stories from the Cornell Nabokov Festival, ed. G. Gibian and S. J.
Parker (Ithaca, NY, 1984), p. 51.

9 Vladimir Nabokov, *Speak, Memory: An Autobiography Revisited*
(New York, 1999), pp. 215–16.

10 *Strong Opinions*, p. 139.

11 Ibid., p. 189.

12 See Don Barton Johnson, '"Terror": Pre-Texts and Post-Texts', in *A
Small Alpine Form: Studies in Nabokov's Short Fiction*, ed. C. Nicol and
G. Barabtarlo (New York, 1993), pp. 46–54.

13 *Collected Stories*, p. 173.

14 Ibid., pp. 176–7.

15 Ibid., pp. 177–8.

16 *Rul´*, 20 May 1923, p. 13.

17 Vladimir Nabokov, *Bend Sinister* (New York, 1990), p. 175.

18 *Collected Stories*, p. 176.

19 Johnson, '"Terror": Pre-Texts and Post-Texts', p. 53.

20 *Speak, Memory*, p. 9.

21 Vladimir Nabokov, *Nikolai Gogol* (New York, 1961), p. 145.

22 Vladimir Nabokov, 'The Creative Writer', *Bulletin of New England
Modern Language Association*, IV/1 (1942), p. 25. The essay was subse-
quently revised and republished as 'The Art of Literature and
Commonsense' in *Lectures on Literature* (London, 1981), pp. 371–80.

23 *Collected Stories*, pp. 149, 153.

24 Ibid., pp. 28, 26, 31.

25 Nabokov's angel resembles the demon in Mikhail Vrubel's illustrations for the 1890/91 edition of Lermontov's poem: 'A great painter
treated his "Demon" in quite a different way and in terms of such
peacock colors amid diamond-blazing eyes and purple clouds that
Lermontov's genius ought to sleep content.' Vladimir Nabokov, 'The
Lermontov Mirage', *The Russian Review*, I/1 (1941), p. 32. He was to
make direct allusions to Vrubel across his work. See Gerard de Vries
and D. Barton Johnson, *Nabokov and the Art of Painting* (Amsterdam,
2006), pp. 106–8, and Gavriel Shapiro, *The Sublime Artist's Studio:
Nabokov and Painting* (Evanston, IL, 2009), pp. 127–8.

26 Vladimir Nabokov, 'Natasha', trans. Dmitri Nabokov, *The New Yorker*
(9 June 2008), at www.newyorker.com/fiction/features/2008/06/
09/080609fi_fiction_nabokov.

27 Vladimir E. Alexandrov, *Nabokov's Otherworld* (Princeton, NJ, 1991), p. 4.

28 Vladimir Nabokov, 'Rupert Bruk', *Grani* (1922), pp. 211–31. For commentary, see Don Barton Johnson, 'Vladimir Nabokov and Rupert Brooke', in *Nabokov and His Fiction: New Perspectives*, ed. Julian W. Connolly (Cambridge, 1999), pp. 177–96, and Alexandrov, ed., *The Garland Companion*, pp. 733–4.

29 Johnson, 'Vladimir Nabokov and Rupert Brooke', pp. 185–6.

30 Ibid., p. 193.

31 Gennady Barabtarlo, 'Jack in the Suitcase (*Revenge*)', in *Aerial View: Essays on Nabokov's Art and Metaphysics* (New York, 1993), p. 16.

32 Julian W. Connolly, *Nabokov's Early Fiction: Patterns of Self and Other* (Cambridge, 1992), p. 16.

33 *Collected Stories*, p. 15.

34 Ibid., p. 136, 133.

35 B. Boyd and R. M. Pyle, eds, *Nabokov's Butterflies: Unpublished and Uncollected Writings* (London, 2000), p. 649.

36 From a 1927 poem, 'In Paradise', in ibid., p. 123.

37 *Collected Stories*, p. 136.

38 Ibid., p. 647.

39 Boyd, *The Russian Years*, p. 236.

40 Brian Boyd, 'New Light on Nabokov's Russian Years', *Cycnos*, x/1 (1993), at http://revel.unice.fr/cycnos/document.html?id=1281.

41 *King, Queen, Knave*, pp. vi, v, vi.

42 *Nikolai Gogol*, p. 70. See also, *Strong Opinions* pp. 100–1.

43 Vladimir Nabokov, 'Philistines and Philistinism', in *Lectures on Russian Literature* (London, 1983), p. 313.

44 *King, Queen, Knave*, p. 10.

45 Ibid., pp. 200, 138.

46 *Strong Opinions*, p. 95.

47 *King, Queen, Knave*, p. 1.

48 Ibid., pp. 20, 21, 27, 24.

49 Ibid., pp. 227–8.

50 *Collected Stories*, p. 648.

51 Gleb Struve, 'Notes on Nabokov as a Russian Writer', *Wisconsin Studies*, VIII/2 (1967), p. 154.

52 Alexandrov, ed., *The Garland Companion*, p. 203.

53 Boyd, *The Russian Years*, p. 93.

54 Writing in *Mir isskustva* in 1902 and 1898 respectively. John E. Bowlt, *Moscow and St Petersburg in Russia's Silver Age, 1900–1920* (London, 2008), p. 69.

55 Alexandrov, *Nabokov's Otherworld*, p. 219.

56 V. Nabokov, *The Gift* (London, 1981), p. 159.

57 Michael Basker, 'Introduction' to Nikolay Gumilyov, *The Pillar of Fire: Selected Poems* (London, 1999), p. 26.

58 Alexandrov, *Nabokov's Otherworld*, p. 215.

59 *Strong Opinions*, p. 168.

60 Boyd, *The Russian Years*, p. 289 and *Speak, Memory*, p. 229.

61 Boyd, *The Russian Years*, pp. 290, 291.

62 John Updike, *New Republic* (26 September 1964), pp. 15–18.

63 Vladimir Nabokov, *The Luzhin Defense* (London, 1994), pp. 34, 249, 246, 252.

64 Luzhin's suicide echoes that of a German chess master, Curt von Bardeleben, who jumped to his death from a Berlin window in 1924. Coincidentally, the Nabokovs rented rooms from a relative of his, a General von Bardeleben, at 27 Luitpoldstrasse from August 1929 until early 1932. See Vladimir Nabokov, *Glory* (London, 1974), pp. 7–8. Another chess grandmaster, Akiba Rubinstein, withdrew from a game in 1932 because of a schizophrenic episode. Like Luzhin, he suffered from anthropophobia, a fear of people and society.

65 *Strong Opinions*, p. 163.

66 Alfred Appel, Jr, *Nabokov's Dark Cinema* (New York and Oxford, 1974), p. 155.

67 *Strong Opinions*, p. 45.

68 Alexandrov, *Nabokov's Otherworld*, p. 85.

69 Vladislav Khodasevich, 'Luzhin's Defense', *Vozrozhdenie* (11 October 1930), translated by Jeff Edmunds, at www.libraries.psu.edu/nabokov /khodas.htm.

70 Boyd, *The Russian Years*, p. 343.

71 Ludmila A. Foster, 'Nabokov in Russian Émigré Criticism', *Russian Literature Triquarterly*, 3 (1973), pp. 333, 337.

72 Alexandrov, ed., *The Garland Companion*, p. 134.

73 Vladimir Nabokov, *The Eye* (London, 1992), p. 9.

74 Ibid., pp. 31, 35.

75 Connolly, *Nabokov's Early Fiction*, p. 78.

76 *The Eye*, pp. 102–3.

77 Alexandrov, ed., *The Garland Companion*, p. 133.

78 See *The Eye*, pp. 58–9.

79 See Don Barton Johnson, 'That Butterfly in Nabokov's *Eye*', *Nabokov Studies*, 4 (1997), pp. 10–11.

80 *The Eye*, p. 77.

81 Ibid., p. 103.

82 Ibid., p. 10.

83 Vladimir Nabokov, 'Good Readers and Good Writers', in *Lectures on Literature*, p. 3.

84 Vladimir Nabokov, *The Annotated Lolita*, edited by Alfred Appel, Jr (London, 1995), p. 315.

85 Matthew J. Bruccoli and Dmitri Nabokov, eds, *Vladimir Nabokov: Selected Letters, 1940–77* (London, 1991), p. 209.

86 See Boyd, *The Russian Years*, p. 363. Nabokov singled out Conrad Veidt as one of his favourite actors. See Appel, Jr, *Nabokov's Dark Cinema*, p. 137.

87 Alexandrov, ed., *The Garland Companion*, p. 393.

88 S. Karlinsky, ed., *Dear Bunny, Dear Volodya: The Nabokov-Wilson Letters, 1940–1971* (Berkeley and Los Angeles, CA, 2001), p. 331.

89 *Strong Opinions*, p. 10.

90 Karlinsky, ed., *Nabokov-Wilson Letters*, p. 331.

91 Alexandrov, ed., *The Garland Companion*, p. 393.

92 Boyd, *The Russian Years*, p. 351.

3 Sirin, Part Two: *Glory* to *The Gift*

1 Vladimir Nabokov, 'The Lermontov Mirage', *The Russian Review*, I/1 (1941), p. 34.

2 Brian Boyd, *Vladimir Nabokov: The Russian Years* (London, 1993), p. 377.

3 Ibid, p. 382.

4 Vladimir Nabokov, *Glory* (London, 1974), p. 8.

5 Andrew Field, *Nabokov: His Life in Part* (London, 1977), p. 158.

6 Vladimir Nabokov, *Strong Opinions* (New York, 1973), p. 88.

7 Ibid., p. 193.

8 *Glory*, p. 66.

9 A literal translation of the novel's Russian title, *Podvig*, is 'exploit'.

10 *Glory*, pp. 120, 9.

11 Ibid., pp. 11, 29. See also Pekka Tammi's commentary in Vladimir E. Alexandrov, ed., *The Garland Companion to Vladimir Nabokov* (New York, 1995), pp. 169–78.

12 *Glory*, p. 11.

13 Ibid., p. 16.

14 See Boyd, *The Russian Years*, p. 48 and Vladimir Nabokov, *Speak, Memory: An Autobiography Revisited* (New York, 1999), pp. 62–3.

15 Alexandrov, ed., *The Garland Companion*, p. 175.

16 *Glory*, pp. 188, 187, 74.

17 Alexandrov, ed., *The Garland Companion*, pp. 169–70.

18 Boyd, *The Russian Years*, p. 360.

19 Leona Toker, *Nabokov: The Mystery of Literary Structures* (Ithaca, NY and London, 1989), p. 89.

20 Vladimir Nabokov, *Laughter in the Dark* (New York, 2006), p. vii.

21 Alfred Appel, Jr, *Nabokov's Dark Cinema* (New York and Oxford, 1974), pp. 258–9. For commentary, see Barbara Wyllie, *Nabokov at the Movies: Film Perspectives in Fiction* (Jefferson, NC, 2003), pp. 68–75.

22 Matthew J. Bruccoli and Dimitri Nabokov, eds, *Vladimir Nabokov: Selected Letters, 1940–77* (London, 1991), p. 537.

23 Boyd, *The Russian Years*, p. 363.

24 Ibid., p. 376. The German actor Fritz Kortner subsequently bought an option on *Kamera obskura* in the late 1930s. See Appel, Jr, *Nabokov's Dark Cinema*, p. 137.

25 For more, see Wyllie, *Nabokov at the Movies*.

26 Boyd, *The Russian Years*, p. 374.

27 Ibid., p. 378.

28 Alexandrov, ed., *The Garland Companion*, p. 88.

29 Vladimir Nabokov, *Despair* (New York, 1966), p. xiii.

30 Ibid., p. xi.

31 Neil Cornwell, '*Otchaianie* [*Despair* (English Edition 1966)]', *The Literary Encyclopedia* (24 November 2008), at www.litencyc.com/php/sworks.php?rec=true&UID=3006.

32 'The Lermontov Mirage', p. 34.

33 William C. Carroll, 'The Cartesian Nightmare of *Despair*', in *Nabokov's Fifth Arc: Nabokov and Others on His Life and Work*, ed. J. E. Rivers and C. Nicol (Austin, TX, 1982), p. 86.

34 Alexander Pushkin, *The Queen of Spades and Other Stories* (London, 1987), p. 179.

35 Nabokov described the 'mediocre and overrated' Dostoevsky as a progenitor of 'melodramatic muddle and phoney mysticism'. *Strong Opinions*, p. 226.

36 Julian W. Connolly, *Nabokov's Early Fiction: Patterns of Self and Other* (Cambridge, 1992), p. 78.

37 See Carroll, 'The Cartesian Nightmare of *Despair*', pp. 94–5.

38 Don Barton Johnson, 'Sources of Nabokov's *Despair*', in *Nabokov at Cornell*, ed. G. Shapiro (Ithaca, NY, 2003), p. 11.

39 *Despair*, p. 193.

40 'Sources of Nabokov's *Despair*', pp. 16 and 10–12. Barton Johnson also cites two other similar and highly publicized cases, one British and another German, that occurred at the same time.

41 Connolly, *Nabokov's Early Fiction*, p. 157.

42 See Alexandrov, ed., *The Garland Companion*, p. 100, n. 14 and Avril Pyman, *A History of Russian Symbolism* (Cambridge, 1994), p. 290 and *passim*.

43 Carroll, 'The Cartesian Nightmare of *Despair*', pp. 88–93.

44 Oscar Wilde, *The Picture of Dorian Gray* (London, 2003), p. 203.

45 *Despair*, p. 121.

46 Vladimir Nabokov, *Lectures on Literature* (San Diego, CA, 1980), p. 376.

47 Connolly, *Nabokov's Early Fiction*, p. 151.

48 *Despair*, p. 62.

49 Ibid., pp. 70, 177, 172.

50 Boyd, *The Russian Years*, p. 394.

51 *Speak, Memory*, p. 232.

52 Ibid.

53 Ibid., p. 10.

54 Vladimir Nabokov, *Collected Stories* (London, 2001), p. 658.

55 Boyd, *The Russian Years*, p. 405.

56 *Collected Stories*, p. 303.

57 Ibid., p. 286.

58 Ibid., p. 296.

59 Ibid., pp. 347, 346 (my emphasis).

60 Ibid., p. 83.

61 Ibid., pp. 83, 84, 79.

62 *Strong Opinions*, p. 68.

63 Vladimir Nabokov, 'Exile', in *Nabokov's 'Invitation to a Beheading':
A Critical Companion*, ed. Julian W. Connolly (Evanston, IL, 1997),
p. 152.

64 Vladimir Nabokov, *Invitation to a Beheading* (London, 1963), p. 7.

65 *Strong Opinions*, p. 287.

66 Ibid., p. 1.

67 *Lectures on Literature*, p. 376.

68 *Strong Opinions*, pp. 58, 76.

69 *Invitation to a Beheading*, pp. 21, 61.

70 Ibid., p. 5. Attributed to 'the melancholy, extravagant, wise, witty,
magical, and altogether delightful Pierre Delalande, whom I invented'
(p. 8).

71 Ibid., pp. 182, 175, 102.

72 Ibid., p. 103.

73 Ibid., pp. 115–16.

74 Toker, *The Mystery of Literary Structures*, p. 127.

75 *Invitation to a Beheading*, p. 76.

76 Gennady Barabtarlo, *Aerial View: Essays on Nabokov's Art and
Metaphysics* (New York, 1993), p. 28.

77 An Eyed Hawk Moth, first featured in chapter 9. *Bend Sinister*
(London, 1974), pp. xix, 240–41.

78 B. Boyd and R. M. Pyle, eds, *Nabokov's Butterflies: Unpublished and
Uncollected Writings* (London, 2000), p. 649.

79 *Invitation to a Beheading*, p. 80.

80 Vladimir Nabokov, *Pnin* (London, 1960), p. 17.

81 *Bend Sinister*, p. 174.

82 *Lectures on Literature*, p. 378.

83 *Invitation to a Beheading*, p. 115.

84 Connolly, ed., *Nabokov's 'Invitation to a Beheading'*, p. 28.

85 *Invitation to a Beheading*, p. 7.

86 Connolly, ed., *Nabokov's 'Invitation to a Beheading'*, p. 5.

87 Boyd, *The Russian Years*, p. 421.

88 Andrei Graf in *Novoe slovo* (March 1938), cited in Maxim D. Shrayer, *The World of Nabokov's Stories* (Austin, TX, 1999), p. 135.

89 Stacy Schiff, *Véra (Mrs Vladimir Nabokov): Portrait of a Marriage* (New York, 1999), p. 77.

90 Boyd, *The Russian Years*, p. 435.

91 Ibid., p. 486.

92 Ibid., p. 480.

93 Schiff, *Véra*, p. 86.

94 Boyd, *The Russian Years*, p. 433.

95 Ibid.

96 Matthew J. Bruccoli and Dmitri Nabokov, eds, *Vladimir Nabokov: Selected Letters 1940–77* (London, 1991), p. 26.

97 Schiff, *Véra*, pp. 89, 87.

98 Boyd, *The Russian Years*, p. 441.

99 Neil Cornwell, *Vladimir Nabokov* (Plymouth, 1999), p. 56. Nabokov had read *Ulysses* in 1931. On Nabokov and Joyce, see Neil Cornwell, *James Joyce and the Russians* (Basingstoke, 1992), pp. 71–9.

100 Vladimir Nabokov, *The Gift* (London, 1981), p. 332.

101 Ibid., pp. 299, 79, 91.

102 Ibid., pp. 88–9, 136, 8, 331.

103 Toker, *The Mystery of Literary Structures*, p. 149.

104 For more, see ibid., pp. 150–53.

105 *The Gift*, p. 313.

106 Ibid., pp. 287, 8.

107 *Speak, Memory*, p. 215.

108 *The Gift*, p. 169.

109 See Vladimir E. Alexandrov, *Nabokov's Otherworld* (Princeton, NJ, 1991), pp. 110–11.

110 *The Gift*, p. 169.

111 Ibid., pp. 283, 304, 169.

112 See Don Barton Johnson, *Worlds in Regression: Some Novels of Vladimir Nabokov* (Ann Arbor, MI, 1985), pp. 101–5.

113 *The Gift*, p. 160.

114 Ibid., p. 159.

115 For more, see Toker, *The Mystery of Literary Structures*, pp. 161–2.

116 *The Gift*, p. 333. For more detailed commentary, see Alexander Dolinin,

'*The Gift*', in *The Garland Companion*, ed. Alexandrov, pp. 159–65.

117 *The Gift*, p. 331.

118 *Speak, Memory*, p. 14.

119 *Strong Opinions*, p. 69.

4 Looking to Other Shores, 1938–40

1 Feodor Sologub, *The Created Legend* (Teddington, 2006), p. 1.

2 Brian Boyd, *Vladimir Nabokov: The Russian Years* (London, 1993), pp. 504, 492.

3 *The Vladimir Nabokov Research Newsletter*, 10 (1983), p. 46.

4 Vladimir Nabokov, *The Real Life of Sebastian Knight* (London, 1964), pp. 117, 44.

5 Ibid., pp. 14, 172, 173.

6 Lara Delage-Toriel, 'Disclosures under Seal: Nabokov, Secrecy and the Reader', *Cycnos*, xxiv/1 (2006), at http://revel.unice.fr/cycnos/document.html?id=1048.

7 Vladimir Nabokov, 'Pouchkine ou le vrai et le vraisemblable', *La Nouvelle Revue Française* (1937), translated by Dmitri Nabokov as 'Pushkin, or the Real and the Plausible', *The New York Review of Books*, xxxv/5 (31 March 1988), p. 40, at www.nybooks.com/articles/4480.

8 For more, see Will Norman, '*The Real Life of Sebastian Knight* and the Modernist Impasse', *Nabokov Studies*, x/1 (2006), pp. 67–97.

9 Matthew J. Bruccoli and Dmitri Nabokov, eds, *Vladimir Nabokov: Selected Letters, 1940–77* (London, 1991), p. 117.

10 *The Real Life of Sebastian Knight*, p. 151.

11 '. . . the snowflakes we see / are the germ cells of stars and the sea life to be.' Vladimir Nabokov, 'The Refrigerator Awakes' (1942), in *Poems and Problems* (New York, 1970), p. 153.

12 For commentary, see '*The Real Life of Sebastian Knight*: An Introduction to Central Modes', in Dabney Stuart, *Nabokov: The Dimensions of Parody* (Baton Rouge, LA, 1978), pp. 1–33; Anthony Olcott, 'The Author's Special Intention: A Study of *The Real Life of Sebastian Knight*', in *A Book of Things About Vladimir Nabokov*, ed. Carl Proffer (Ann Arbor, MI, 1974), pp. 104–21, and J. B. Sisson, '*The Real Life of Sebastian Knight*', in Vladimir E. Alexandrov, ed.,

The Garland Companion to Vladimir Nabokov (New York, 1995), pp. 633–43.

13 See Don Barton Johnson, *Worlds in Regression: Some Novels of Vladimir Nabokov* (Ann Arbor, MI, 1985), p. 22.

14 Gerard de Vries and Don Barton Johnson, *Nabokov and the Art of Painting* (Amsterdam, 2006), pp. 40–41.

15 Ibid., p. 41.

16 *The Real Life of Sebastian Knight*, pp. 162, 171, 170.

17 Ibid., p. 6.

18 For more, see Boyd, *The Russian Years*, pp. 496, 501–2 and Susan Elizabeth Sweeney, 'Postscript to A Purloined Letter', in *The Nabokovian*, 29 (1992), pp. 38–41.

19 Vladimir Nabokov, *Strong Opinions* (New York, 1973), p. 24.

20 See Priscilla Meyer, 'Black and Violet Words: *Despair* and *The Real Life of Sebastian Knight* as Doubles', *Nabokov Studies*, 4 (1997), pp. 37–60.

21 *Strong Opinions*, p. 86.

22 Boyd, *The Russian Years*, p. 504.

23 For more, see Yuri Leving, 'Singing *The Bells* and *The Covetous Knight*: Nabokov and Rachmaninoff's Operatic Translations of Poe and Pushkin', in *Transitional Nabokov*, ed. W. Norman and D. White (Bern, 2009), pp. 206–7.

24 Vladimir Nabokov, *The Enchanter*, trans. Dmitri Nabokov (New York, 1986), p. xv.

25 See Neil Cornwell, *Vladimir Nabokov* (Plymouth, 1999), p. 58.

26 David M. Bethea, 'Sologub, Nabokov, and the Limits of Decadent Aesthetics', *The Russian Review*, 63 (January 2004), p. 50.

27 Alexander Dolinin, 'Nabokov's Time Doubling: From *The Gift* to *Lolita*', *Nabokov Studies*, 2 (1995), p. 19, n. 45.

28 See Vladimir Nabokov, *The Gift* (London, 1981), pp. 172–3.

29 Vladimir Nabokov, *The Collected Stories* (London, 2001), p. 648.

30 *The Enchanter*, pp. xvi, xx.

31 Gennady Barabtarlo, *Aerial View: Essays on Nabokov's Art and Metaphysics* (New York, 1993), p. 41.

32 *The Enchanter*, p. 25.

33 Ibid., pp. 15–16.

34 See Barabtarlo, *Aerial View*, pp. 54–68.

35 *The Enchanter*, p. 72.

36 Barabtarlo, *Aerial View*, p. 51.

37 Dmitri Nabokov, 'On a Book Entitled *The Enchanter*', in *The Enchanter*, p. 106.

38 Ibid., p. xvii.

39 D. Nabokov, 'On a Book Entitled *The Enchanter*', ibid., p. 87.

40 *Collected Stories*, p. 658.

5 Becoming Vladimir Nabokov: *Bend Sinister* to *Lolita*

1 Vladimir Nabokov, *Strong Opinions* (New York, 1973), p. 98.

2 Andrew Field, *Nabokov: His Life in Part* (London, 1977), p. 232.

3 Ibid., p. 234.

4 Brian Boyd, *Vladimir Nabokov: The American Years* (London, 1993), p. 18.

5 S. Karlinsky, ed., *Dear Bunny, Dear Volodya: The Nabokov-Wilson Letters, 1940–1971* (Berkeley and Los Angeles, CA, 2001), pp. 1–2.

6 *Strong Opinions*, p. 5.

7 Boyd, *The American Years*, p. 26.

8 Karlinsky, ed., *Nabokov-Wilson Letters*, p. 50.

9 For more, see Leving 'Singing *The Bells* and *The Covetous Knight*'.

10 B. Boyd and R. M. Pyle, eds, *Nabokov's Butterflies: Unpublished and Uncollected Writings* (London, 2000), p. 297.

11 Nabokov commemorated the find with a poem, 'A Discovery'. See *Poems and Problems* (New York, 1970), pp. 155–6.

12 Boyd, *The American Years*, pp. 32, 71.

13 Published as *Three Russian Poets* (1945), and *Nikolai Gogol* (1944).

14 For more, see Kurt Johnson and Steven L. Coates, *Nabokov's Blues: The Scientific Odyssey of a Literary Genius* (Cambridge, MA, 1999).

15 *Strong Opinions*, pp. 315–16. The location was to inspire both the heroine's name and the final scenes of *Lolita*.

16 Vladimir Nabokov, *Bend Sinister* (New York, 1990), p. xi.

17 Boyd, *The American Years*, p. 59.

18 See Karlinsky, ed., *Nabokov-Wilson Letters*, pp. 95–8.

19 Ibid., p. 83.

20 Boyd, *The American Years*, pp. 303, 469, 82.

21 Vladimir Nabokov, *The Annotated Lolita*, ed. Alfred Appel, Jr (London, 1995), pp. 316–17.

22 Field, *His Life in Part*, p. 250.

23 *Poems and Problems*, p. 105.

24 Boyd, *The American Years*, p. 36.

25 Vladimir Nabokov, *Speak, Memory: An Autobiography Revisited* (New York, 1999), p. 195.

26 *Strong Opinions*, p. 100.

27 Boyd, *The American Years*, p. 22.

28 Andrew Field, *VN: The Life and Art of Vladimir Nabokov* (London, 1987), p. 235.

29 *Strong Opinions*, pp. 10, 192, 98.

30 For more, see Nabokov's comments to Edmund Wilson in *Nabokov-Wilson Letters*, p. 173. On Neuengamme, see *Holocaust Encyclopedia*, United States Holocaust Memorial Museum, at www.ushmm.org/wlc/article.php?lang=en&ModuleId=10005539.

31 Brian Boyd, *Vladimir Nabokov: The Russian Years* (London, 1993), p. 70.

32 See *Poems and Problems*, p. 153.

33 *Bend Sinister*, p. xi.

34 Matthew J. Bruccoli and Dmitri Nabokov, eds, *Vladimir Nabokov: Selected Letters, 1940–77* (London, 1991), p. 48.

35 *Bend Sinister*, p. xiii.

36 Ibid., pp. xii–xiv.

37 Quoted in Leona Toker, *Nabokov: The Mystery of Literary Structures* (Ithaca, NY and London, 1989), p. 178.

38 *Nabokov-Wilson Letters*, p. 223.

39 *Strong Opinions*, p. 33.

40 *Bend Sinister*, p. 233.

41 Ibid., p. 241.

42 Ibid., pp. 241, 1.

43 Ibid., p. 240.

44 *Speak, Memory*, p. 215.

45 *Bend Sinister*, p. xv.

46 Vladimir Nabokov, *Nikolai Gogol* (New York, 1961), p. 149.

47 See *Bend Sinister*, pp. xiv–xvii; Don Barton Johnson, *Worlds in Regression: Some Novels of Vladimir Nabokov* (Ann Arbor, MI, 1985), pp. 187–205; Toker, *The Mystery of Literary Structures*, pp. 177–97; Leona Toker, 'Between Allusion and Coincidence: Nabokov, Dickens

and Others', *Hebrew University Studies in Literature and the Arts*, XII/2 (1984), pp. 175–198, and Lucy Maddox, *Nabokov's Novels in English* (Athens, GA, 1983), pp. 50–65.

48 Bruccoli and Nabokov, eds, *Selected Letters*, p. 49.

49 *Bend Sinister*, p. 233.

50 Boyd, *The American Years*, p. 307.

51 Gennady Barabtarlo, *Phantom of Fact: A Guide to Nabokov's 'Pnin'* (Ann Arbor, MI, 1989), p. 19.

52 Vladimir Nabokov, *Pnin* (London, 1960), pp. 22, 7, 127, 43, 160, 155.

53 Julian W. Connolly, '*Pnin*: The Wonder of Recurrence and Transformation', in *Nabokov's Fifth Arc: Nabokov and Others on His Life's Work*, ed. J. E. Rivers and C. Nicol (Austin, TX, 1982), p. 195.

54 Bruccoli and Nabokov, eds, *Selected Letters*, pp. 156–7.

55 Connolly, 'The Wonder of Recurrence', p. 195.

56 *Speak, Memory*, p. 215.

57 *Pnin*, p. 46.

58 Ibid., p. 74.

59 For more, see Gerard de Vries, 'The Vane Sisters', *The Literary Encyclopedia* (29 August 2007), at www.litencyc.com/php/sworks.php?rec=true&UID=21898; Boyd, *The American Years*, pp. 192–5, and Barbara Wyllie, *Nabokov at the Movies: Film Perspectives in Fiction* (Jefferson, NC, 2003), pp. 165–6.

60 *Pnin*, p. 81.

61 Ibid., p. 80.

62 Ibid., pp. 132, 73, 105 (see *Nabokov-Wilson Letters*, p. 303), 113.

63 From the original *New Yorker* version, which Nabokov subsequently cut. See Barabtarlo, *Phantom of Fact*, p. 40.

64 Boyd, *The American Years*, p. 201.

65 Appel, Jr, ed., *The Annotated Lolita*, p. 289. See also Alexander Dolinin, 'What Happened to Sally Horner?: A Real-Life Source of Nabokov's *Lolita*', *Zembla*, at www.libraries.psu.edu/nabokov/dolilol.htm.

66 Chaplin was one of Nabokov's favourite movie comedians, along with Buster Keaton, the Marx Brothers, Laurel & Hardy and Harold Lloyd. See *Strong Opinions*, pp. 163–4.

67 David Shipman, 'OBITUARY: Lita Grey', *The Independent* (4 January 1996), at http://findarticles.com/p/articles/mi_qn4158/is_19960104/ai_n9632851.

68 Bill Delaney, 'Nabokov's *Lolita*', *The Explicator*, LVI/2 (1998),
    p. 99. Chaplin called her 'my "Age of Innocence" girl'. When Humbert
    bribes Lolita to fondle him under the desk in her schoolroom, they
    are overlooked by Reynolds's painting (see Appel, Jr, ed., *The Annotated
    Lolita*, p. 198). Humbert also considers growing a Chaplinesque tooth-
    brush moustache, ibid., p. 48.

69 Shipman, 'OBITUARY: Lita Grey'.

70 Appel, Jr, ed., *The Annotated Lolita*, pp. 120, 316, 323, 39, 15. Ironically,
    Lolita's surname also puns with the Hays Code, the rigid moral guide-
    lines that came into force across the American film industry in 1934.
    These stipulated, amongst other things, that seduction and rape 'are
    never the proper subject for comedy' (II, 3b); 'Sex perversion or any
    inference to it is forbidden' (3c), and 'Apparent cruelty to children or
    animals' is 'repellent' (XII, 5).

71 Bruccoli and Nabokov, eds, *Selected Letters*, p. 144.

72 Lance Olsen, *Lolita: A Janus Text* (New York, 1995), p. 15.

73 Bruccoli and Nabokov, eds, *Selected Letters*, p. 198.

74 Herbert Gold in *The Achievements of Vladimir Nabokov: Essays, Studies,
    Reminiscences and Stories from the Cornell Nabokov Festival*, ed. G. Gibian
    and S. J. Parker (Ithaca, NY, 1984), pp. 58–9.

75 Boyd, *The American Years*, p. 365.

76 Ibid., pp. 365, 366.

77 *Strong Opinions*, p. 20.

78 *Nabokov-Wilson Letters*, p. 330. For commentary on Nabokov's ethics,
    see Leland de la Durantaye, *Style is Matter: The Moral Art of Vladimir
    Nabokov* (Ithaca, NY, 2007), and Michael Wood, *The Magician's
    Doubts: Nabokov and the Risks of Fiction* (London, 1994).

79 Bruccoli and Nabokov, eds, *Selected Letters*, p. 185.

80 Vladimir Nabokov, 'What Is This Evil Deed' (1959), *Poems and
    Problems*, p. 147. Nabokov deliberately echoes a stanza from Boris
    Pasternak's poem, 'Nobel Prize', in which Pasternak protests at having
    been ostracized by the Russian cultural community following his
    receipt of the award in 1958: 'Am I a gangster or murderer? / Of what
    crime do I stand / Condemned? I made the whole world weep / At
    the beauty of my land.' Boris Pasternak, *Selected Poems* (London,
    1983), p. 154.

81 Stanley Weintraub, *Beardsley* (London, 1972), p. 238.

82 Olsen, *Lolita: A Janus Text*, p. 95. For more commentary, see 'The *Lolita* Phenomenon', in Neil Cornwell, *Vladimir Nabokov* (Plymouth, 1999), pp. 57–72.

83 Ibid., p. 64.

84 Appel, Jr, ed., *The Annotated Lolita*, p. 4.

85 *Strong Opinions*, p. 26.

86 Appel, Jr, ed., *The Annotated Lolita*, pp. 119, 180.

87 See Christina Teckiner, 'Time in *Lolita*', *Modern Fiction Studies*, 25 (1979), pp. 463–9; *The Mystery of Literary Structures*, pp. 209–16; Barbara Wyllie, '"Guilty of Killing Quilty": The Central Dilemma of Nabokov's *Lolita*?', *Slovo*, VIII/1 (1995), pp. 12–16. For a counterargument, see Brian Boyd, '"Even Homais Nods": Nabokov's Fallibility, or, How to Revise *Lolita*', *Nabokov Studies*, 2 (1995), pp. 60–85. For John Ray, Jr's role, see George Ferger, 'Who's Who in the Sublimelight: "Suave John Ray" and Lolita's "Secret Points"', *Nabokov Studies*, 8 (2004), pp. 137–98.

88 Appel, Jr, ed., *The Annotated Lolita*, p. 316.

89 *Strong Opinions*, p. 115.

90 For more on Poe and others, see Carl R. Proffer, *Keys to Lolita* (Bloomington, IN, 1968).

91 Gerard de Vries and D. Barton Johnson, *Nabokov and the Art of Painting* (Amsterdam, 2006), p. 64.

92 Appel, Jr, ed., *The Annotated Lolita*, p. 56.

93 De Vries and Johnson, *Nabokov and the Art of Painting*, p. 64.

94 Appel, Jr, ed., *The Annotated Lolita*, pp. 250 and 251.

95 Ibid., pp. 258, 259.

96 Savely Senderovich and Yelena Shvarts, 'The Juice of Three Oranges: An Exploration in Nabokov's Language and World', *Nabokov Studies*, 1 (2000), p. 85. See also J. Douglas Clayton, *Pierrot in Petrograd: Commedia dell'Arte/Balagan in Twentieth-Century Russian Theatre and Drama* (Montreal, 1993), and Olga Soboleva, *The Silver Mask: Harlequinade in the Symbolist Poetry of Blok and Belyi* (Bern, 2008).

97 *Strong Opinions*, p. 171. See also Susan Elizabeth Sweeney, 'Looking at the Harlequins: Nabokov, the World of Art and the Ballets Russes', in *Nabokov's World*, vol. II: *Reading Nabokov*, ed. J. Grayson, A. McMillin and P. Meyer (Basingstoke, 2002), pp. 73–95.

98 Senderovich and Shvarts, 'The Juice of Three Oranges', p. 88.

99 Vladimir Nabokov, *Look at the Harlequins!* (London, 1980), p. 13.

100 Appel, Jr, ed., *The Annotated Lolita*, p. 32.

101 *Pnin*, p. 132.

102 See Appel, Jr, ed., *The Annotated Lolita*, pp. 299, 301, 448, n. 301/5, 405, n. 201/5, 201.

103 See, for example, 'The Fourth Dimension', and 'The Marvels of Space and Time', in Maurice Maeterlinck, *The Life of Space*, trans. Bernard Miall (London, 1928).

104 Maurice Maeterlinck, 'The Tragical in Daily Life', in *The Treasure of the Humble*, trans. Alfred Sutro (New York, 1903), p. 111.

105 Appel, Jr, ed., *The Annotated Lolita*, p. 250.

106 Ibid., p. 162.

107 Vladimir Nabokov, *The Gift* (London, 1981), p. 105.

108 Appel, Jr, ed., *The Annotated Lolita*, p. 292.

109 Ibid., pp. 293, 308.

110 Ibid., pp. xxx, 201, 272, 278.

111 Ibid., p. 277.

112 *Strong Opinions*, p. 168.

113 Appel, Jr, ed., *The Annotated Lolita*, p. 13.

114 Ibid., p. 134.

115 Thomas R. Frosch, 'Parody and Authenticity in *Lolita*', in *Vladimir Nabokov: Modern Critical Views*, ed. Harold Bloom (New York, 1987), p. 127.

116 *Speak, Memory*, p. 169.

117 Appel, Jr, ed., *The Annotated Lolita*, p. 49.

118 Ibid., pp. 309, 129.

119 Vladimir E. Alexandrov, *Nabokov's Otherworld* (Princeton, NJ, 1991), p. 186.

120 Vladimir Nabokov, *King, Queen, Knave* (London, 1993), p. vi.

121 *Strong Opinions*, p. 15.

122 Bruccoli and Nabokov, eds, *Selected Letters*, p. 140.

123 From Stevenson's *Essays in the Art of Writing*, noted by Nabokov in *Lectures on Literature* (San Diego, CA, 1980), p. 180.

6 World Fame: Hollywood and Switzerland, 1958–68

1 Vladimir Nabokov, *Strong Opinions* (New York, 1973), p. 106.
2 Brian Boyd, *Vladimir Nabokov: The American Years* (London, 1993), p. 369.
3 They were published in 1958 and 1960 respectively.
4 See B. Boyd and R. M. Pyle, eds, *Nabokov's Butterflies: Unpublished and Uncollected Writings* (London, 2000), pp. 528–37.
5 Stacy Schiff, *Véra (Mrs Vladimir Nabokov): Portrait of a Marriage* (New York, 1999), p. 258.
6 Ibid., p. 259.
7 Alfred Appel, Jr, *Nabokov's Dark Cinema* (New York and Oxford, 1974), p. 236.
8 Schiff, *Véra*, p. 269.
9 Appel, Jr, *Nabokov's Dark Cinema*, p. 58.
10 S. Karlinsky, ed., *Dear Bunny, Dear Volodya: The Nabokov-Wilson Letters, 1940–1971* (Berkeley and Los Angeles, CA, 2001), p. 366.
11 Vladimir Nabokov, *Lolita: A Screenplay* (New York, 1974), p. ix.
12 Boyd, *The American Years*, p. 408.
13 Ibid. See also Appel, Jr, *Nabokov's Dark Cinema*, pp. 232–4.
14 Richard Corliss, *Lolita* (London, 1994), p. 19.
15 *Lolita: A Screenplay*, p. xii.
16 For commentary, see '*Lolita*: Kubrick in Nabokovland', in Thomas Allen Nelson, *Kubrick: Inside a Film Artist's Maze* (Bloomington, IN, 1982), pp. 54–78; Barbara Wyllie, 'Nabokov and Cinema', in *The Cambridge Companion to Nabokov*, ed. Julian W. Connolly (Cambridge and New York, 2005), pp. 218–19; and Lara Delage-Toriel, *Lolita de Vladimir Nabokov et de Stanley Kubrick* (Nantes, 2009).
17 Nevertheless, Nabokov found the slapstick sequence featuring 'the collapsing cot' at The Enchanted Hunters, and 'the frills of Miss Lyon's elaborate nightgown' 'painful'. *Lolita: A Screenplay*, p. xiii.
18 *Strong Opinions*, p. 55.
19 Ibid., p. 35.
20 Ibid., p. 55.
21 Jay Arnold, 'The Design of *A Tale of a Tub* (with a Digression on a Mad Modern Critic)', *ELH*, XXX/2 (1966), p. 222.
22 Boyd, *The American Years*, p. 416.

23 Vladimir Nabokov, 'Problems of Translation: *Onegin* in English', *Partisan Review* (1955), repr. in R. Schulte and J. Biguenet, *Theories of Translation: An Anthology of Essays from Dryden to Derrida* (Chicago, IL, 1992), p. 143.

24 Arnold, 'The Design of *A Tale of a Tub*', p. 222.

25 Vladimir Nabokov, *Pale Fire* (London, 1991), p. 71.

26 Arnold, 'The Design of *A Tale of a Tub*', p. 206. Kinbote is the alter ego of V. Botkin, the true author of his book, whose name, partially anagrammaticized as *nikto* means, in Russian, 'nothing'.

27 Vladimir Nabokov, *Speak, Memory: An Autobiography Revisited* (New York, 1999), p. 227.

28 Ibid., p. 160.

29 *Strong Opinions*, p. 11.

30 *Pale Fire*, p. 106.

31 Ibid., pp. 248, 208.

32 Boyd, *The American Years*, p. 463.

33 *Pale Fire*, p. 53, ll. 808–10.

34 Ibid., p. 227.

35 *Speak, Memory*, p. 227.

36 John Stark, *The Literature of Exhaustion: Borges, Nabokov, and Barth* (Durham, NC, 1974), p. 64.

37 For commentary, see Priscilla Meyer, *Find What the Sailor Has Hidden: Vladimir Nabokov's 'Pale Fire'* (Middletown, CT, 1988); Neil Cornwell, *Vladimir Nabokov* (Plymouth, 1999), pp. 73–84; Gerard de Vries, Nabokov's *Pale Fire* and the Romantic Movement', *Zembla*, at http://libraries.psu.edu/nabokov/devriespf.htm, and 'Nabokov's Game of Worlds', in Robert Alter, *Partial Magic: The Novel as Self-Conscious Genre* (Berkeley and Los Angeles, CA, 1975), pp. 180–217.

38 Arnold, 'The Design of *A Tale of a Tub*', pp. 218–19.

39 *Pale Fire*, pp. 61 and 247.

40 Ibid., p. 205. See *Worlds in Regression*, pp. 71–3. According to the OED, a 'bodkin' is 'a person wedged in between two others where there is proper room for two only'.

41 *Pale Fire*, p. 152.

42 *Strong Opinions*, p. 170.

43 See Brian Boyd, *Nabokov's 'Pale Fire': The Magic of Artistic Discovery* (Princeton, NJ, 1999), pp. 133–7.

44 *Pale Fire*, pp. 43 (ll. 489–90), 76 and 173.

45 Ibid., pp. 240, 138, 39, ll. 357–8.

46 Ibid., p. 34, ll. 178–9.

47 *Speak, Memory*, p. 6.

48 *Pale Fire*, p. 45, ll. 541–4.

49 Ibid., p. 48, ll. 648–52.

50 See John Burt Foster, Jr, *Nabokov's Art of Memory and European Modernism* (Princeton, NJ, 1993), p. 223, and Meyer, *Find What the Sailor Has Hidden*, pp. 131–2.

51 *Pale Fire*, p. 227.

52 Ibid., p. 29, ll. 1–2.

53 Ibid., p. 14.

54 Ibid., pp. 14–15.

55 Mary McCarthy, 'A Bolt from the Blue', in *Pale Fire*, p. v.

56 Vladimir Nabokov, *The Gift* (London, 1981), p. 159.

57 *Pale Fire*, p. 91.

58 Vladimir Nabokov, *Invitation to a Beheading* (London, 1963), p. 165.

59 *Pale Fire*, p. 231.

60 Ibid., p. 29, l. 4.

61 *Speak, Memory*, p. 19.

62 Ibid., p. 106.

63 See Brian Boyd, *Vladimir Nabokov: The Russian Years* (London, 1993), pp. 7–8.

64 Boyd, *The American Years*, p. 460.

65 *Strong Opinions*, p. 28.

66 Boyd and Pyle, eds, *Nabokov's Butterflies*, p. 613.

67 Boyd, *The American Years*, p. 517.

68 *Strong Opinions*, p. xv.

69 Ibid., pp. 20, 62.

70 Apart from *The Gift* (1963) and *The Defense* (1964), which were translated by Michael Scammell, *Mary* (1970), by Michael Glenny and 'A Russian Beauty', by Simon Karlinsky (all overseen by Nabokov).

71 See Matthew J. Bruccoli and Dmitri Nabokov, eds, *Vladimir Nabokov: Selected Letters, 1940–77* (London, 1991), pp. 361–6.

72 Boyd, *The American Years*, p. 459.

73 Schiff, *Véra*, p. 291.

74 Andrew Field, *Nabokov: His Life in Part* (London, 1977), p. 23.

75 Schiff, *Véra*, p. 291.

76 Boyd, *The American Years*, p. 471.

77 Interview for CBC radio, 20 March 1973, quoted in Dmitri Nabokov, 'Translating with Nabokov', in *The Achievements of Vladimir Nabokov: Essays, Studies, Reminiscences and Stories from the Cornell Nabokov Festival*, ed. G. Gibian and S. J. Parker (Ithaca, NY, 1984), p. 146.

78 Edmund Wilson, 'The Strange Case of Pushkin and Nabokov', *The New York Review of Books*, IV/12 (15 July 1965), at www.nybooks.com/articles/12829.

79 *Strong Opinions*, p. 206. See also Karlinsky, ed., *Nabokov-Wilson Letters*, p. 27 and Bruccoli and Nabokov, eds, *Selected Letters*, pp. 273–4.

80 Karlinsky, ed., *Nabokov-Wilson Letters*, p. 366.

81 Vladimir Nabokov, 'Letters: The Strange Case of Nabokov and Wilson', *The New York Review of Books*, V/2 (26 August 1965), at www.nybooks.com/articles/12795.

82 Karlinsky, ed., *Nabokov-Wilson Letters*, p. 372.

83 See ibid., pp. 373–4.

84 Vladimir Nabokov, *Ada or Ardor: A Family Chronicle* (London, 1971), p. 9.

85 See Roy Arthur Swanson, 'Nabokov's *Ada* as Science Fiction', *Science Fiction Studies*, II/1 (1975), at www.depauw.edu/sfs/backissues/5/swanson5art.htm.

86 L. N. Tolstoy, *Anna Karenin*, trans. K. Zinovieff (Richmond, 2008), p. 3.

87 For commentary, see Brian Boyd, *Nabokov's 'Ada': The Place of Consciousness*, 2nd edn (Christchurch, NZ, 2002); Robert Alter, '*Ada*, or The Perils of Paradise', in *Vladimir Nabokov: Modern Critical Views*, ed. Harold Bloom (New York, 1987), pp. 175–89, and Don Barton Johnson, *Worlds in Regression: Some Novels of Vladimir Nabokov* (Ann Arbor, MI, 1985), pp. 51–9, 116–34.

88 *Ada*, p. 460.

89 Harvey Breit, 'Talk With Mr Nabokov', *The New York Times*, 18 February 1951, at www.nytimes.com/books/97/03/02/lifetimes/nab-v-talk.html.

90 *Ada*, p. 221.

91 Ibid., p. 459.

92 Charles Nicol, 'Ada or Disorder', in *Nabokov's Fifth Arc: Nabokov and Others on His Life's Work*, ed. J. E. Rivers and C. Nicol (Austin, TX, 1982), p. 230.

93 *Ada*, pp. 22–3.

94 *Lolita: A Screenplay*, p. 3.

95 *Strong Opinions*, pp. 120, 146.

96 Ibid., p. 193.

97 *Ada*, p. 63.

98 Ibid., pp. 124–5.

99 See ibid., p. 442.

100 *Speak, Memory*, pp. 15–16, 242, 95–6.

101 *Ada*, p. 441.

102 *Lectures on Literature* (San Diego, CA, 1980), p. 260.

103 *Ada*, pp. 437, 431.

104 For more, see Marina Grishakova, *The Models of Space, Time and Vision in V. Nabokov's Fiction: Narrative Strategies and Cultural Frames* (Tartu, 2006), esp. pp. 72–80.

105 *Ada*, p. 420.

106 Vladimir Nabokov, *Bend Sinister* (New York, 1990), pp. 173–4.

107 *Strong Opinions*, p. 184.

108 *Ada*, p. 440.

109 Lucy Maddox, *Nabokov's Novels in English* (Athens, GA, 1983), p. 115.

110 *Bend Sinister*, pp. 173–4.

111 *Ada*, p. 420; *Strong Opinions*, pp. 185–6.

112 *Ada*, p. 443.

113 Field, *His Life in Part*, p. 87.

114 *Speak, Memory*, p. 56.

115 *Ada*, p. 428.

116 Michael Seidel, 'Stereoscope: Nabokov's *Ada* and *Pale Fire*', in *Vladimir Nabokov: Modern Critical Views*, ed. Bloom, p. 240.

117 *Ada*, p. 422.

118 Ibid., p. 335.

119 *Strong Opinions*, p. 186.

120 *Ada*, p. 200.

121 *Strong Opinions*, p. 186.

7 The Final Arc, 1969–77

1 Vladimir Nabokov, *Strong Opinions* (New York, 1973), p. 11.
2 Vladimir E. Alexandrov, ed., *The Garland Companion to Vladimir Nabokov* (New York, 1995), p. 3.
3 Maurice Couturier, 'Nabokov in Postmodernist Land', *Critique*, XXXIV/4 (Summer 1993), p. 247.
4 Ibid., pp. 253–4.
5 Brian Boyd, *Vladimir Nabokov: The American Years* (London, 1993), p. 316. For more on Pynchon, see Susan Elizabeth Sweeney, 'The V-Shaped Paradigm: Nabokov and Pynchon', in *Nabokov at the Crossroads of Modernism and Postmodernism*, *Cycnos*, XII/2 (1995), pp. 173–80.
6 John Stark, *The Literature of Exhaustion: Borges, Nabokov, and Barth* (Durham, NC, 1974), pp. 3–4.
7 Matthew J. Bruccoli and Dmitri Nabokov, eds, *Vladimir Nabokov: Selected Letters, 1940–77* (London, 1991), p. 57.
8 Vladimir Nabokov, *Lectures on Literature* (San Diego, CA, 1980), p. 5.
9 Bruccoli and Nabokov, eds, *Selected Letters*, p. 382.
10 Vladimir Nabokov, *Bend Sinister* (New York, 1990), p. 174.
11 *Strong Opinions*, p. 179.
12 Boyd, *The American Years*, p. 662.
13 *Strong Opinions*, pp. 149–50.
14 Vladimir Nabokov to Donald Cammell, 30 July 1971. See Sam Umland, 'Donald Cammell/Pale Fire Screenplay', *NABOKV-L* (11 February 2009), at http://listserv.ucsb.edu/lsv-cgi-bin/wa?A2=ind0902&L=nabokv-l&T=0&P=4596, and 'PUBLICATION: On Donald Cammell's Adaptation of Pale Fire' (2 March 2009), at http://listserv.ucsb.edu/lsv-cgi-bin/wa?A2=ind0903&L=nabokv-l&T=0&P=1690.
15 Vladimir Nabokov, *Transparent Things* (New York, 1989), p. 48.
16 Ibid., p. 95.
17 See Bruccoli and Nabokov, eds, *Selected Letters*, pp. 115–16 and 285–6; Brian Boyd, *Nabokov's 'Ada': The Place of Consciousness*, 2nd edn (Christchurch, NZ, 2002), and *Vladimir Nabokov's 'Pale Fire': The Magic of Artistic Discovery* (Princeton, NJ, 1999).
18 *Transparent Things*, p. 98.

19 Vladimir Nabokov, *Speak, Memory: An Autobiography Revisited* (New York, 1999), p. 106.

20 *Transparent Things*, pp. 13, 2.

21 Vladimir Nabokov, *Pale Fire* (London, 1991), p. 45.

22 Vladimir Nabokov, *The Collected Stories* (London, 2001), p. 340.

23 *Transparent Things*, pp. 19, 52, 103.

24 Vladimir Nabokov, *Look at the Harlequins!* (London, 1980), p. 26.

25 Vladimir Nabokov, *The Annotated Lolita*, ed. Alfred Appel, Jr, p. 297.

26 Vladimir Nabokov, *Pnin* (London, 1960), p. 58.

27 *Pale Fire*, p. 45.

28 *Transparent Things*, p. 104.

29 Vladimir Nabokov, *The Gift* (London, 1981), p. 283.

30 *Pnin*, p. 17.

31 *Lectures on Literature*, p. 377.

32 Vladimir Nabokov, *Ada or Ardor: A Family Chronicle* (London, 1971), p. 389; *Speak, Memory*, p. 10.

33 *Pnin*, p. 49.

34 *Transparent Things*, p. 93.

35 Boyd, *The American Years*, p. 610. See also Bruccoli and Nabokov, eds, *Selected Letters*, pp. 513, 515–19, 544–5.

36 Boyd, *The American Years*, p. 619.

37 Ibid., p. 616.

38 For commentary, see ibid., pp. 623–42; Alexandrov, ed., *The Garland Companion*, pp. 330–40; Neil Cornwell, *Vladimir Nabokov* (Plymouth, 1999), pp. 101–16; Don Barton Johnson, *Worlds in Regression: Some Novels of Vladimir Nabokov* (Ann Arbor, MI, 1985), pp. 135–53 and 170–84, and Lucy Maddox, *Nabokov's Novels in English* (Athens, GA, 1983), pp. 142–59.

39 *Look at the Harlequins!*, p. 76.

40 Johnson, *Worlds in Regression*, p. 173: Vladimir Nabokov, *King, Queen, Knave* (London, 1993), p. vi.

41 *Look at the Harlequins!*, p. 13.

42 Alexandrov, ed., *The Garland Companion*, p. 673.

43 Maddox, *Nabokov's Novels in English*, p. 143.

44 *Look at the Harlequins!*, p. 178.

45 Alexandrov, ed., *The Garland Companion*, p. 340.

46 Boyd, *The American Years*, p. 630.

47 Ibid., pp. 643, 644.

48 Ibid., pp. 653–4; Bruccoli and Nabokov, eds, *Selected Letters* (London, 1979), p. 562.

49 Peter Quennell, ed., *Vladimir Nabokov: A Tribute* (London, 1979), p. 136.

50 *Strong Opinions*, p. 4.

51 Vladimir Nabokov, *The Original of Laura: Dying is Fun (A Novel in Fragments)* (London, 2009), pp. 221, 227.

52 Ibid., pp. 57, 205, 1, 3, 249, 145/245, 171.

53 Vladimir Nabokov, *The Eye* (London, 1992), p. 55.

54 *Speak, Memory*, p. 14.

55 *Strong Opinions*, pp. 9–10.

56 Ibid., pp. 28, 181, 107.

57 Alden Whitman, 'Vladimir Nabokov, 72 Today, Writing a New Novel', *The New York Times* (23 April 1971), at www.nytimes.com/books/97/03/02/lifetimes/nab-v-newnovel.html.

Select Bibliography

Works

Ada or Ardor: A Family Chronicle (London, 1971)
The Annotated Lolita, ed. A. Appel, Jr (London, 1995)
Bend Sinister (London, 1974)
The Collected Stories (London, 1997)
Conclusive Evidence (New York, 1951)
Despair (London, 1981); *Otchaianie* (Berlin, 1936)
Drugie berega (*Other Shores*) (New York, 1954)
The Enchanter, trans. D. Nabokov (London, 1986)
Eugene Onegin: A Novel in Verse, 2 vols (Princeton, NJ, 1990)
The Eye (London, 1992); *Sogliadatei* (Paris, 1930)
The Gift (London, 1981); *Dar* (Paris, 1937–8; New York, 1952)
Glory (London, 1974); *Podvig* (Paris, 1932)
Invitation to a Beheading (London, 1963); *Priglashenie na kazn´*
    (Paris, 1938)
King, Queen, Knave (London, 1993); *Korol´, dama, valet* (Berlin, 1928)
Laughter in the Dark (New York, 1978); *Kamera obskura* (Paris, 1933)
Lectures on Literature (London, 1981)
Lectures on Russian Literature (London, 1982)
Lolita (New York, 1997)
Lolita: A Screenplay (New York, 1997)
Look at the Harlequins! (London, 1980)
The Luzhin Defense (London, 1994); *Zashchita Luzhina* (Berlin, 1930)
The Man from the USSR and Other Plays (San Diego, CA, 1985)
Mary (London, 1973); *Mashen´ka* (Berlin, 1926)
Nikolai Gogol (New York, 1961)

The Original of Laura: Dying is Fun (A Novel in Fragments) (London, 2009)
Pale Fire (London, 1991)
Pnin (London, 1960)
Poems and Problems (New York, 1970)
The Real Life of Sebastian Knight (London, 1964)
*Sobranie sochinenii russkogo perioda v piati tomakh: stoletie so dnia
    rozhdeniia, 1899–1999*, ed. N. I. Artemenko-Tolstoi and A. A. Dolinin
    (St Petersburg, 1999)
Speak, Memory: An Autobiography Revisited (New York, 1999)
Stikhi (Ann Arbor, MI, 1979)
Strong Opinions (New York, 1973)
'Tragediia gospodina Morna'; Pesy; Lektsii o drame (St Petersburg, 2008)
Transparent Things (New York, 1972)
Verses and Versions: Three Centuries of Russian Poetry, ed. B. Boyd,
    S. Shvabrin (New York, 2008)

Lepidoptery

Boyd, Brian, and Robert Michael Pyle, eds, *Nabokov's Butterflies:
    Unpublished and Uncollected Writings* (London, 2000)
Johnson, Kurt, and Steven L. Coates, *Nabokov's Blues: The Scientific Odyssey
    of a Literary Genius* (Cambridge, MA, 1999)
Zimmer, Dieter E., *A Guide to Nabokov's Butterflies and Moths* (Hamburg,
    2001)

Letters

Bruccoli, Matthew J., and Dmitri Nabokov, eds, *Vladimir Nabokov: Selected
    Letters, 1940–77* (London, 1991)
Karlinsky, Simon, ed., *Dear Bunny, Dear Volodya: The Nabokov-Wilson
    Letters, 1940–1971* (Berkeley and Los Angeles, CA, 2001)

Biography

Boyd, Brian, *Vladimir Nabokov: The American Years* (London, 1993)
—, *Vladimir Nabokov: The Russian Years* (London, 1993)
Grayson, Jane, *Vladimir Nabokov* (London, 2001)
Schiff, Stacy, *Véra (Mrs Vladimir Nabokov): Portrait of a Marriage*
    (New York, 1999)

Criticism

Alexandrov, Vladimir E., ed., *The Garland Companion to Vladimir Nabokov*
    (New York, 1995)
—, *Nabokov's Otherworld* (Princeton, NJ, 1991)
Appel, Alfred Jr, *Nabokov's Dark Cinema* (New York and Oxford, 1974)
Appel, Alfred Jr, and Charles Newman, eds, *Nabokov: Criticism,
    Reminiscences, Translations and Tributes* (London, 1970)
Barabtarlo, Gennady, *Aerial View: Essays on Nabokov's Art and Metaphysics*
    (New York, 1993)
—, *Phantom of Fact: A Guide to Nabokov's 'Pnin'* (Ann Arbor, MI, 1989)
Blackwell, Stephen H., *Zina's Paradox: The Figured Reader in Nabokov's 'Gift'*
    (New York, 2000)
Bloom, Harold, ed., *Vladimir Nabokov: Modern Critical Views* (New York,
    1987)
—, ed., *Vladimir Nabokov's 'Lolita'* (New York, 1987)
Boyd, Brian, *Nabokov's 'Ada': The Place of Consciousness*, 2nd edn
    (Christchurch, NZ, 2002)
—, *Vladimir Nabokov's 'Pale Fire': The Magic of Artistic Discovery*
    (Princeton, NJ, 1999)
Connolly, Julian W., ed., *The Cambridge Companion to Nabokov*
    (Cambridge, 2005)
—, *Nabokov's Early Fiction: Patterns of Self and Other* (Cambridge, 1992)
—, *Nabokov and His Fiction: New Perspectives* (Cambridge, 1999)
—, *Nabokov's 'Invitation to a Beheading': A Critical Companion* (Evanston,
    IL, 1997)
Corliss, Richard, *Lolita* (London, 1994)
Cornwell, Neil, *Vladimir Nabokov* (Plymouth, 1999)

Delage-Toriel, Lara, *Lolita de Vladimir Nabokov et de Stanley Kubrick* (Nantes, 2009)

De Vries, Gerard, and Donald Barton Johnson, *Nabokov and the Art of Painting* (Amsterdam, 2006)

Dolinin, Aleksandr, *Istinnaia zhizn´ pisatelia Sirina: Raboty o Nabokove* (St Petersburg, 2004)

Durantaye, Leland de la, *Style is Matter: The Moral Art of Vladimir Nabokov* (Ithaca, NY, 2007)

Field, Andrew, *Nabokov: His Life in Art* (London, 1967)

—, *Nabokov: His Life in Part* (London, 1977)

Foster, John Burt Jr, *Nabokov's Art of Memory and European Modernism* (Princeton, NJ, 1993)

Gibian, George, and Stephan Jan Parker, eds, *The Achievements of Vladimir Nabokov: Essays, Studies, Reminiscences and Stories from the Cornell Nabokov Festival* (Ithaca, NY, 1984)

Glynn, Michael, *Vladimir Nabokov: Bergsonian and Russian Formalist Influences in His Novels* (Basingstoke, 2007)

Grayson, Jane, *Nabokov Translated: A Comparison of Nabokov's Russian and English Prose* (Oxford, 1977)

Grayson, Jane, Arnold McMillin and Priscilla Meyer, eds, *Nabokov's World*, 2 vols (Basingstoke, 2002)

Grishakova, Marina, *The Models of Space, Time and Vision in V. Nabokov's Fiction: Narrative Strategies and Cultural Frames* (Tartu, 2006)

Holabird, Jean, *Vladimir Nabokov: Alphabet in Color* (Corte Madera, CA, 2005)

Johnson, Donald Barton, *Worlds in Regression: Some Novels of Vladimir Nabokov* (Ann Arbor, MI, 1985)

Juliar, Michael, *Vladimir Nabokov: A Descriptive Bibliography* (New York, 1986)

Kellman, Steven G., and Irving Malin, eds, *Torpid Smoke: The Stories of Vladimir Nabokov* (Amsterdam, 2000)

Larmour, David H. J., ed., *Discourse and Ideology in Nabokov's Prose* (New York and London, 2002)

Leving, Iurii, *Vokzal – garazh – angar: Vladimir Nabokov i poetika russkogo urbanizma* (St Petersburg, 2004)

Maddox, Lucy, *Nabokov's Novels in English* (London, 1983)

Meyer, Priscilla, *Find What the Sailor Has Hidden: Vladimir Nabokov's 'Pale Fire'* (Middletown, CT, 1988)

Naumann, Marina T., *Blue Evenings in Berlin: Nabokov's Short Stories of the 1920s* (New York, 1978)

Nicol, Charles, and Gennady Barabtarlo, eds, *A Small Alpine Form: Studies in Nabokov's Short Fiction* (New York, 1993)

Norman, Will, and Duncan White, eds, *Transitional Nabokov* (Bern, 2009)

Olsen, Lance, *Lolita: A Janus Text* (New York, 1995)

Packman, David, *Vladimir Nabokov: The Structure of Literary Desire* (Columbia, MO, 1982)

Page, Norman, ed., *Vladimir Nabokov: The Critical Heritage* (London and New York, 1982)

Pifer, Ellen, *Nabokov and the Novel* (Cambridge, MA, 1980)

—, ed., *Vladimir Nabokov's 'Lolita': A Casebook* (Oxford and New York, 2003)

Proffer, Carl R., ed., *A Book of Things About Vladimir Nabokov* (Ann Arbor, MI, 1974)

—, *Keys to Lolita* (Bloomington, IN, 1968)

Quennell, Peter, ed., *Vladimir Nabokov: A Tribute* (London, 1979)

Rampton, David, *Vladimir Nabokov: A Critical Study of the Novels* (Cambridge, 1984)

Rivers, J. E., and Charles Nicol, eds, *Nabokov's Fifth Arc: Nabokov and Others on His Life's Work* (Austin, TX, 1982)

Shapiro, Gavriel, *Delicate Markers: Subtexts in Vladimir Nabokov's 'Invitation to a Beheading'* (New York, 1998)

—, ed., *Nabokov at Cornell* (Ithaca, NY, 2003)

—, *The Sublime Artist's Studio: Nabokov and Painting* (Evanston, IL, 2009)

Shrayer, Maxim D., *The World of Nabokov's Stories* (Austin, TX, 1999)

Stark, John, *The Literature of Exhaustion: Borges, Nabokov, and Barth* (Durham, NC, 1974)

Stuart, Dabney, *Vladimir Nabokov: The Dimensions of Parody* (Baton Rouge, LA, 1978)

Tammi, Pekka, *Problems of Nabokov's Poetics: A Narratological Analysis* (Helsinki, 1985)

—, *Russian Subtexts in Vladimir Nabokov's Fiction: Four Essays* (Tampere, 1999)

Toker, Leona, *Nabokov: The Mystery of Literary Structures* (Ithaca, NY, 1989)

Vickers, Graham, *Chasing Lolita: How Popular Culture Corrupted Nabokov's Little Girl All Over Again* (Chicago, IL, 2008)

Wood, Michael, *The Magician's Doubts: Nabokov and the Risks of Fiction* (London, 1994)

Wyllie, Barbara, *Nabokov at the Movies: Film Perspectives in Fiction* (Jefferson, NC, 2003)

Zunshine, Lisa, *Nabokov at the Limits: Redrawing Critical Boundaries* (New York, 1999)

Online

Ada Online
www.ada.auckland.ac.nz/

The Gift Project
http://giftconcordance.pbworks.com/

Nabokov Bibliography
www.vnbiblio.com/

Nabokov Online Journal
www.nabokovonline.com

Nabokov Under Glass
www.nypl.org/research/chss/epo/nabokov/fintro.htm

Zembla
www.libraries.psu.edu/nabokov/zembla.htm

Acknowledgements

I would like to thank everyone who has read and commented on drafts of this book, especially Eva Wittenberg, Neil Cornwell, Lara Delage-Toriel and Miranda Jackson. I would also like to thank Vlasta Gyenes at the UCL SSEES Library for her invaluable help in obtaining for me a variety of hard-to-find critical sources, and UCL SSEES for its support of this project. Finally, I am greatly indebted to Dmitri Nabokov for his permission to use images from the Nabokov Estate.

A modified version of the Library of Congress system of transliteration has been used throughout. Exceptions include established English spellings of Russian names (e.g. Dostoevsky, Chernyshevsky, Rachmaninov), names like Fyodor, where a 'y' is used to indicate proper pronunciation, and names as they appear in the English versions of Nabokov's work.

Excerpts from Nabokov's works appear by permission of the Estate of Vladimir Nabokov.